DOCUMENTED
BRIEFING

D1537901

Navy/OSD Collaborative Review of Acquisition Policy for DoD C3I and Weapon Programs

Daniel Gonzales, Eric Landree, John Hollywood, Steven Berner, Carolyn Wong

Prepared for the United States Navy and the Office of the Secretary of Defense

NATIONAL DEFENSE RESEARCH INSTITUTE

The research described in this report was prepared for the United States Navy and the Office of the Secretary of Defense (OSD). The research was conducted in the RAND National Defense Research Institute, a federally funded research and development center sponsored by the OSD, the Joint Staff, the Unified Combatant Commands, the Department of the Navy, the Marine Corps, the defense agencies, and the defense Intelligence Community under Contract W74V8H-06-C-0002.

The RAND Corporation is a nonprofit research organization providing objective analysis and effective solutions that address the challenges facing the public and private sectors around the world. RAND's publications do not necessarily reflect the opinions of its research clients and sponsors.

RAND® is a registered trademark.

Published 2007 by the RAND Corporation
1776 Main Street, P.O. Box 2138, Santa Monica, CA 90407-2138
1200 South Hayes Street, Arlington, VA 22202-5050
4570 Fifth Avenue, Suite 600, Pittsburgh, PA 15213-2665
RAND URL: http://www.rand.org/
To order RAND documents or to obtain additional information, contact
Distribution Services: Telephone: (310) 451-7002;
Fax: (310) 451-6915; Email: order@rand.org

Preface

This briefing summarizes research that reviews current U.S. Department of Defense (DoD) policy governing the development of integrated command, control, communication, and intelligence (C3I) and weapon systems. Our focus is on interoperability and information assurance (IA) policy in the context of DoD acquisition and requirement policy. This review was conducted to identify ambiguities, conflicts, overlaps, and shortfalls in DoD policy and to recommend solutions for clarifying policy and remedying other shortcomings that were found.

This research should be of interest to DoD personnel who are responsible for formulating, reviewing, or implementing DoD policy pertaining to the development and upgrade of interoperable C3I and weapon systems.

This research was cosponsored by the Office of the Under Secretary of Defense for Acquisition, Technology, and Logistics (OUSD[AT&L]) and the Assistant Secretary of the Navy, Research, Development, and Acquisition (RDA) Chief Systems Engineer (CHSENG), and conducted within the Acquisition and Technology Policy Center of the RAND National Defense Research Institute, a federally funded research and development center sponsored by the Office of the Secretary of Defense, the Joint Staff, the Unified Combatant Commands, the Department of the Navy, the Marine Corps, the defense agencies, and the defense Intelligence Community.

For more information on the RAND Acquisition and Technology Policy Center, contact the Director, Philip Antón. He can be reached by email at atpc-director@rand.org; by phone at 310-393-0411, extension 7798; or by mail at the RAND Corporation, 1776 Main Street, Santa Monica, California 90407-2138. More information about RAND is available at http://www.rand.org.

Contents

Acknowledgments

This research would not have been possible without the support of Delores M. Etter, Assistant Secretary of the Navy (ASN) for RDA, and Carl Siel, chief systems engineer of the Navy for RDA. We thank them for their support The authors also wish to thank Vitalij Garber, senior technical advisor for interoperability, Office of the Under Secretary of Defense for Acquisition, Technology, and Logistics (OUSD[AT&L]), and Cheryl Walton, director, standards policy and guidelines, Assistant Secretary of the Navy, RDA CHSENG, for their guidance and support of this research.

We thank Patrick M. Kern, global information grid (GIG) senior system engineer, Office of the Assistant Secretary of Defense for Networks and Information Integration (ASD[NII]), and his staff for their assistance in this research.

Finally, we thank David Signori of Evidenced Based Research and our RAND colleague Louis R. Moore for their careful reviews of this briefing.

Abbreviations

ACAT	acquisition category
AEHF	Advanced Extremely High Frequency
AoA	analysis of alternatives
APB	acquisition program baseline
ASD(C3I)	Assistant Secretary of Defense for Command, Control, Communication, and Intelligence
ASD(HD)	Assistant Secretary of Defense for Homeland Defense
ASD(NII)	Assistant Secretary of Defense for Networks and Information Integration
ASN	Assistant Secretary of the Navy
BFT	blue force tracking
C&A	certification and accreditation
C3I	command, control, communication, intelligence
C4	command, control, communication, and computer
CA	certification authority
CAR	capability area review
CBA	capability-based assessment
CDD	capability development document
CEC	cooperative engagement capability
CHSENG	chief systems engineer
CIO	chief information officer
CIP	critical infrastructure protection
CJCSI	Chairman of the Joint Chiefs of Staff instruction
CL	confidentiality level
CND	computer network defense

CNSS	Committee on National Security Systems
COCOM	combatant command
COI	community of interest
CONOPS	concept of operations
COP	common operational picture
COTS	commercial, off the shelf
CPD	capability production document
CPM	capability portfolio management
CRD	capstone requirements document
DAA	designated approval authority
DAB	Defense Acquisition Board
DAPA	Defense Acquisition Performance Assessment
DARPA	Defense Advanced Research Projects Agency
DCI	Director of Central Intelligence
DCID	Director of Central Intelligence Directives
DEPSECDEF	deputy secretary of defense
DIA	Defense Intelligence Agency
DIACAP	Defense Information Assurance Certification Accreditation Program
DISA	Defense Information Systems Agency
DISR	Defense Information Standards Registry
DITSCAP	DoD Information Technology Security Certification and Accreditation Process
DNS	domain name service
DOC	distribution operations center
DoD	U.S. Department of Defense
DoDAF	U.S. Department of Defense architecture framework
DoDI	Department of Defense instruction
DOT&E	Defense Office of Testing and Evaluation
DPS	date processing system
DSB	Defense Science Board
DSP	defense policy and strategy

E2E	end-to-end
FAA	functional area analysis
FCS	Future Combat System
FIA	Future Imagery Architecture
FISMA	Federal Information Security Management Act of 2002 (Public Law 107-347)
FNA	functional needs analysis
FSA	functional solution analysis
GIG	global information grid
I&S	interoperability and supportability
IA	information assurance
IAM	information assurance manager
ICD	initial capability document
IER	information exchange requirement
Int	integrated
IOC	initial operational capability
IP	internet protocol
IPL	integrated priority list
IS	information system
ISP	information support plan
ISSM	information system security management
ITAB	Information Technology Acquisition Board
J6	Directorate for Command, Control, Communications, and Computer Systems of the U.S. Joint Chiefs of Staff
JCD	joint capability document
JCIDS	Joint Capabilities Integration and Development System
JCS	U.S. Joint Chiefs of Staff
JROCM	Joint Requirements Oversight Council memorandum
JS	joint staff
JTRS	Joint Tactical Radio System
JUON	joint urgent operational needs

KIP	key interface profile
KPP	key performance parameter
MAC	mission assurance category
MAIS	major automated information system
MCEB	Military Communications-Electronics Board
MID	management initiative decision
MS	milestone
NCID	net-centric implementation document
NCOW	net-centric operations and warfare
NGA	National Geospatial-Intelligence Agency
NR-KPP	net-ready key performance parameter
NSA	National Security Agency
NSS	National Security Systems
NSSA	national security space acquisition
NSTISSP	National Security Telecommunications and Information System Security Policy
NTIA	National Telecommunication and Information Administration
OT&E	operational test and evaluation
OUSD(AT&L)	Office of the Under Secretary for Acquisition, Technology, and Logistics
OV	operational view
OV-7	operational-view logical data model
PA	performance allocation
PDR	preliminary design review
PIA	program initiation agreement
PKI	public key infrastructure
PM	program manager
PPSM	port, protocol, and service management
QDR	Quadrennial Defense Review
QoS	quality of service
RDA	research, development, and acquisition
SCI	secret compartmentalized information

SE	system engineering
SM	system manager
SOA	service-oriented architecture
SPIRS	Space-Based Infrared System
STA	system threat assessment
SV	system view
SV-2	system-view system communication description
SV-11	system-view physical schema
SYSCOM	system command
SysML	Systems Modeling Language
T&E	test and evaluation
TEMP	test and evaluation master plan
TEN	tactical edge network
TISP	tailored information support plan
TRL	technology readiness level
TSAT	transformational satellite
TV	technical standards view
TV-2	technical standards–view technical standards forecast
UAV	unmanned aerial vehicle
UDOP	user-defined operational picture
UGV	unmanned ground vehicle
UML	Unified Modeling Language
USD	Under Secretary of Defense
USD(C)	Under Secretary of Defense Comptroller
USD(I)	Under Secretary of Defense for Intelligence
USD(L)	Under Secretary of Defense for Logistics
USD(Policy)	Under Secretary of Defense for Policy
WG	working group

CHAPTER ONE

Introduction

NATIONAL DEFENSE RESEARCH INSTITUTE

IMPROVING DOD POLICY GOVERNING ACQUISITION OF C3I AND WEAPON PROGRAMS

Sponsored by
Assistant Secretary of the Navy RDA CHSENG
OUSD(AT&L)

This briefing summarizes the results of a research project cosponsored by the Office of the Under Secretary of Defense for Acquisition, Technology, and Logistics (OUSD[AT&L]) and the Assistant Secretary of the Navy, Research, Development, and Acquisition (RDA) Chief Systems Engineer (CHSENG).

This briefing was presented to Vitalij Garber, senior technical advisor for interoperability, OUSD(AT&L); and Cheryl Walton, director, standards policy and guidelines, Assistant Secretary of the Navy, RDA CHSENG, on June 20, 2006.

This briefing reflects the conditions of the U.S. Department of Defense (DoD) acquisition environment at the time the analysis was performed and, unless otherwise noted, does not take into consideration changes that have occurred since June 2006.

Purpose

- Identify ambiguities, conflicts, overlaps, and shortfalls in current policies and recommend solutions in
  - Joint Capabilities Integration and Development System (JCIDS)
  - acquisition
  - IT system interoperability and supportability
  - net-centric implementation documents (NCIDs)
  - information assurance (IA)

- Focus – interoperability policy statements in DoD policy

RAND   2

The purpose of the project is to review current DoD policy governing the development and upgrade of interoperable command, control, communication, and intelligence (C3I) and weapon systems. Our focus, therefore, is those elements of DoD policy that pertain to the IT component of these programs.[1] We reviewed this policy area to identify ambiguities, conflicts, overlaps, and shortfalls in these policies and to recommend solutions for clarifying the ambiguities, mitigating the shortfalls, filling the gaps, and resolving the conflicts we found in the policy statements.

We examined five policy areas that apply to the interoperability of C3I and weapon systems. We started by looking at the requirement-gathering process. The current process is governed by requirement policy as defined in the Joint Capabilities Integration and Development System (JCIDS) documentation. Next, we reviewed DoD acquisition policy as determined by DoD 5000–series documentation, as well as several recent studies of the acquisition system that identify where current policy may be deficient and can be improved. Following acquisition, we turned our focus to examining interoperability and supportability policy that has been developed and recently revised specifically for IT systems. Next, we examined a new policy area designed to enhance and ensure the effective integration of global information grid (GIG) component programs so they perform effectively as an end-to-end (E2E) system of systems. Policies in this new area are in the net-centric implementation documents (NCIDs). Finally, we examine information assurance (IA) policy.

---

[1]   Specifically, we focused on weapon programs with high IT content.

Background

- **What is interoperability?**

- **Several interoperability definitions exist**

- **DoD uses architectural approach to defining and achieving interoperability**
  - **Current bottom-up process inhibits efficient development of a single, integrated architecture that summarizes DoD interoperability requirements**

- **Program manager task has become more challenging because of the growing complexity of interoperability guidance**

RAND   3

Interoperability in the broadest sense is a measure of the degree to which various organizations or individuals can operate together effectively. The U.S. Joint Chiefs of Staff (JCS) define *interoperability* as the ability of systems, units, or forces to provide services to and accept services from other systems, units, or forces and to use the services so exchanged to enable them to operate effectively together (JCS, 1994 [1999]).

Interoperability can be achieved by standardization, integration, and cooperation in the development, configuration, training, and use of systems to support operations and to command and control joint and coalition forces.

An essential element of interoperability is system interoperability, which is the ability of two or more systems or components to exchange information and to use the information that has been exchanged (IEEE Computer Society, 1990).

Joint and coalition interoperability needs for specific systems and military units are context dependent. To capture the operational, system, and technology contexts for new system development, DoD has adopted an architectural approach. An architectural approach is also dictated by U.S. law (based on the former Clinger-Cohen Act) (Public Law 104-106). The architecture discloses operational, system, and technical information and dependencies needed to demonstrate interoperability. Consequently, current DoD policy states that program managers (PMs) need specific architecture products to analyze the interoperability and supportability of warfighting capability. Approval of the analysis is used in program milestone review decision. Thus, interoperability requirements of a new system in DoD can be described through the use of operational, system, and technical architectural views or products. The PM's task, however, has recently become more complex and challenging because of additional amplifying interoperability guidance that DoD has established and because of the growing complexity of this guidance.

The current DoD architectural approach to interoperability has shortcomings for the PM and the department as a whole. PMs frequently have to develop their own architecture products for individual systems because the current DoD architecture process has not produced the context architecture products they need to conduct the analysis. Additionally, DoD uses a bottom-up architectural development process. This bottom-up approach can result in much duplication of effort across the entire acquisition system and thus make the development of a single, integrated architecture that summarizes DoD interoperability requirements difficult to achieve. After completion of this research, DoD started development of a new architectural approach for GIG that includes top-down guidance and architecture product data standards, which may reduce the burden on PMs. (See Appendix A for further discussion of integrated architectures).

Approach

- **Examine applicable DoD policies and decompose them into key elements**

- **Summarize and diagram policies, identifying major provisions and interrelationships**
    - **Management structures**
    - **Specified documentation program managers, others called upon to deliver**
    - **Subject-matter topics**
    - **Process specifications**

- **Identify ambiguities, conflicts, and shortfalls in the policies**
    - **Missing elements crucial to policy implementation**

RAND   4

In this analysis of DoD policy, we decomposed policies into their key moving parts. Appendix B lists the policies we examined. We summarized these policies and, in particular, identified their major provisions, management structures, who is responsible for what aspects of policy implementation, the subject matter covered, and the processes that are specified to accomplish the policy goals. As a part of this analysis and decomposition, we also performed a cross-policy analysis to identify ambiguities, conflicts, shortfalls, and missing elements that might be crucial to policy implementation. As the following slides show, we explored selected areas in greater detail to illuminate key issues.

Outline

- JCIDS

- Acquisition

- Interoperability

- NCIDs

- IA

- Summary

RAND   5

The JCIDS policy statements are contained in the DoD 3170 series of documents. We summarize our findings for JCIDS policy documentation in the next two slides.

JCIDS – 3170 Series

- **Description of JCIDS processes and products can be ambiguous**
  - **CBA and acquisition-related processes never discussed or diagrammed jointly**
  - **Not clear what products are expected at each stage of CBA (FAA, FNA, FSA), much less what those products should look like**
  - **Unclear how CBAs relate to programs already in progress or deployed at time JCIDS was created**
  - ***Recommendation*: Address above in next policy revision, using "best" CBA and systems documentation submitted to date as examples**
    - **Example end-to-end process diagram on next slide**

- **Traceability of capability needs across documents unclear**
  - **Indirect linkage between needs coming from COCOMs (IPLs, lessons learned, etc.), JCDs, and other documents**
  - **Indirect linkages between requirements in operational documents (JCD, ICD) and program development documents (CDD, CPD)**
  - ***Recommendation*: Directly require linkages from COCOM needs to JCDs and other documents and audit whether COCOM needs are being addressed on a regular schedule**

RAND

6

We found two major issues with the JCIDS process with respect to interoperability policy. The first is that JCIDS processes and products are described ambiguously. The 3170 series describes two separate processes—one for performing capability-based assessments (CBAs) and one for system acquisition decisions. Though the 3170 series clearly states that the acquisition process is described in the 5000 series, it also states that there is a relationship between the two. The two are never discussed or diagrammed jointly, making it difficult to determine exactly how CBA products relate to acquisition-related products. Within the CBA process, it is not clear what products are expected as deliverables from each stage of the analysis (functional area analysis [FAA], functional needs analysis [FNA], and functional solution analysis [FSA]), much less what the content of those products should be. In response, we recommend clarifying how CBA and acquisition processes relate to each other and describing the products expected at each stage of the CBA process. We also recommend that the JCS provide a set of examples for the best CBA and system documentation submitted to date. The examples can serve to inform PMs on acceptable means of satisfying the JCIDS policy guidance.

The second major issue is a lack of clear traceability across JCIDS and other warfighting needs documents. There is only an indirect link between the needs coming from commanders (integrated priority lists [IPLs], lessons-learned documents) and JCIDS documents such as joint capability documents (JCDs). The former are never mentioned as formal inputs to the JCIDS process, and there are no provisions to trace JCIDS requirements to warfighting needs documents. Within the JCIDS acquisition process, there are only indirect links between the requirements in the early operational documents (JCDs, initial capability documents [ICDs]), and the requirements in the program development documents (capability development documents [CDDs], capability production documents [CPDs]). Again, there is no provision to trace requirements and, in particular, interoperability requirements between these documents and identify which requirements change as successive JCIDS documents are developed. In response, we recommend requiring linkages from combatant command (COCOM) needs documents to JCDs and other JCIDS documents that specifically pertain to interoperability. We also recommend having the JCS perform audits on a regular basis to determine whether priority COCOM needs and interoperability shortfalls are being addressed, whether through nonmateriel or materiel means.

Conceptual JCIDS Relationship to the Acquisition Process

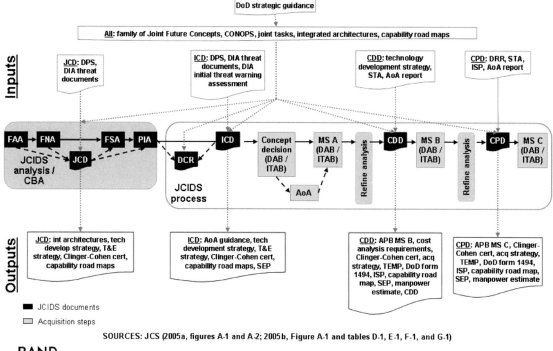

SOURCES: JCS (2005a, figures A-1 and A-2; 2005b, Figure A-1 and tables D-1, E-1, F-1, and G-1)

RAND   7

This slide is a conceptual depiction of what the relationships between the JCIDS CBA and acquisition processes might look like. As shown, the main link between the CBA process and the acquisition-related process appears to be that ICDs should reflect the solutions identified through the FSA and verified through the program initiation agreement (PIA).

The slide also shows the documents that the 3170 series lists as being inputs for each JCIDS document, as well as output documents (i.e., documents that will use the JCIDS document as an input). Some documents are considered to be overarching (DoD Strategic Guidance, Joint Future Concepts and concept of operations [CONOPS], joint tasks, integrated architectures, capability road maps) (DoD, 2004a), and thus influence the preparation of all JCIDS documents. As noted earlier, there are no requirements to consider warfighting needs documents (lessons learned, IPLs) in creating JCIDS documents.

We will see in the next chapter that the acquisition policy documents offer no further guidance on how the JCIDS process relates to the acquisition process.

CHAPTER THREE

Acquisition Policy

Outline

- JCIDS

➡️ • Acquisition

- Interoperability

- NCIDs

- IA

- Summary

RAND   8

We now look at acquisition policy contained in the 5000-series documents.

Acquisition (5000 Series)

- **DoDI 5000 has not been updated in some time, while specific IT system acquisition guidance has evolved more rapidly**
  - **has a single system focus**
  - **discusses interoperability in very general terms**
  - **does not describe Defense Acquisition Board Capability Area Review (DAB CARs)**
  - **does not align acquisition with QDR portfolio management system**

- ***DoD Acquisition Guidebook* (DoD, 2004a) contains more current guidance but is not directive**
  - **contains a global map of related policies and guidance, but is not always clear about which policies are directive**

- **DoD 5000-series guidance is being updated and due to be released later in 2007**

RAND

9

The 5000 series of documentation governs acquisition policy at the top level. DoD Instruction 5000.2 (OUSD[AT&L], 2003), has not been updated since May 12, 2003, while more specific IT system acquisition guidance and interoperability policy has evolved much more rapidly and carries more current dates. A few important points to make about the 5000 series are that this series still has a single-system focus and concentrates on the acquisition system for single programs. It discusses interoperability but only in general terms. This more generic approach to interoperability is not necessarily a drawback of the policy, given the more specific policies that do address interoperability. However, the 5000 series does not address the Defense Acquisition Board (DAB) capability area review (CAR) process that was instituted in recent years to look at the acquisition of systems within a system-of-system context. These new acquisition management elements have been devised in an effort to improve the synchronization of programs that need to be aligned to provide system-of-system capabilities. Therefore, it is important to understand how they fit into the acquisition guidance stated in the DoD 5000 series.

The 5000 series also does not address the recent Quadrennial Defense Review (QDR)–mandated capability portfolio management (CPM) process and the four experiments that are now being undertaken in the department to do capability management using a portfolio approach across a set of programs. The four CPM experiments are in the areas of joint command and control; joint network operations; joint logistics; and battlespace awareness or intelligence, surveillance, and reconnaissance.

It should be noted that the DoD acquisition guidebook is available online (DoD, 2004a) and provides links to a much broader set of policies. However, the guidebook is not directive. It is discretionary and not mandatory guidance, and it contains links to and copies of many policies, some of which are not directive or are in draft form, so it can be confusing for PMs to use.

DoD 5000-series guidance is being updated. The revision of DoDI 5000.2 is under way in the second quarter of FY 2007. The update of DoDD 5000.1 (see DoD, 2006b) is expected to follow the revision of DoDI 5000.2.

Program Acquisition and Management Challenges

- **DoD programs have increasing IT content – computer hardware and software**

- **Key DoD programs with high IT content have encountered significant cost, schedule, and performance problems**
    - higher technology risks than originally estimated for key components
    - Joint Tactical Radio System (JTRS)
    - satellite programs
        - SBIRs
        - FIA
        - AEHF
        - TSAT
    - Army Future Combat System program

- **Joint interoperability and IA requirements have, in many cases, been key design drivers**
    - e.g., JTRS waveforms, DITSCAP certification, software assurance, etc.

RAND

10

Some DoD programs have suffered acquisition setbacks and acquisition management challenges within the past five or six years. These programs, which have suffered the most serious cost growth and schedule slips, appear to have increasing IT content—that is, in terms of total acquisition cost, an increasing percentage of the program deliverable is computer hardware and software.

Key DoD programs with high IT content that have encountered significant problems are some of the core programs for the next generation of C3I systems. These problematic programs include the Joint Tactical Radio System (JTRS) (Feickert, 2005) and a whole assortment of satellite programs, including Space-Based Infrared System (SBIRS), the Future Imagery Architecture (FIA) system, the Advanced Extremely High Frequency (AEHF) program, and the Transformational Satellite (TSAT) system (Hura et al., forthcoming). Another program with high IT content that has suffered some significant cost, schedule, and performance issues is the U.S. Army's Future Combat System (FCS) (Bowman, 2005). These programs are just a few examples of programs with high IT content that have encountered acquisition issues. Many other high–IT content programs exist.

The common theme among all of these programs, and perhaps a source of their problems, is that technology risk appears to have been higher than originally estimated for many key components. Some of the most recent examples of this are the laser communication components associated with TSAT and the technology challenges associated with producing and maturing those technologies.

Another important source of technology risk and program performance risk is joint interoperability and IA requirements. In many cases, joint interoperability and IA requirements have been key design drivers that have resulted in more requirements and more complex requirements being levied on these programs. Examples of such cases include the original 32 software-designed waveforms that the JTRS program was supposed to implement. A second example is the complexity of the DoD Information Technology Security Certification and Accreditation Process (DITSCAP) for IA. A third and recent example is software assurance issues associated with many programs in which higher-cost, domestic software development teams have to be used because less costly overseas software development poses serious software-assurance issues.

Findings of Recent Reviews of the DoD Acquisition System

- **DSB summer study on defense transformation – the acquisition system**
  - **is inflexible and risk averse**
  - **frequently does not deliver systems at cost and on time**
  - **does not allow for rapid technology insertion**
  - **does not adequately address technology risk factors**

- **Defense Acquisition Performance Assessment (DAPA)**
  - **System is slow and overly complex**
  - **DoD 5000 sets Milestone B too early**
    - **Before system design and technology are sufficiently mature to establish high confidence cost, schedule, and performance thresholds**
  - **DoD lacks clearly definable measures of technology readiness**

RAND   11

Two recent studies have reviewed the DoD acquisition system. The first was the Defense Science Board (DSB) summer study on defense transformation (DSB and OUSD[AT&L], 2006). The DSB study concluded that the current acquisition system is inflexible and risk averse. These characteristics result, too frequently, in systems that breach cost and schedule goals. In addition, the current acquisition system does not allow for rapid technology insertion and does not adequately address technology risk.

The second major study was the Defense Acquisition Performance Assessment (DAPA) (Assessment Panel of the Defense Acquisition Performance Assessment Project for the Deputy Secretary of Defense, 2006). The DAPA conclusions were similar to the DSB acquisition study findings, but the DAPA study identified specific sources for defense acquisition shortcomings. For example, the DAPA study found that DoD 5000 policy sets MS B too early in the acquisition process. DAPA asserts that MS B is scheduled before a system is mature enough in its design and technology choices to enable high-confidence cost, schedule, and performance thresholds to be set. In addition, the DAPA study noted that DoD lacked clearly definable technology readiness metrics or technology maturity metrics, thus further hampering its ability to specify a more appropriate placement for MS B in the acquisition cycle.

These findings point toward a need to define technology risk to incorporate the multiple sources from which such risk can stem. Our examples on the previous slide show that technology risk can have roots in technology maturation, as well as other sources such as security considerations. Once an appropriate definition of technology risk has been established and the metrics to measure it have been reviewed and agreed to, acquisition policy can include these establishment technology readiness levels along with associated time-phased goals to help address technology risk.

Recommended Changes to DoD 5000 Series Guidance Specific to High–IT Content Programs*

- **Establish TRLs for key GIG functional areas that affect interoperability**
  - Waveform, communications protocol, and IA functions
  - Quality of Service signaling and protocols, etc.

- **Use GIG TRLs in reviews of GIG and GIG-related programs**
  - Update GIG TRLs based on learning in program reviews

- **Ensure that system designs are reviewed by independent technical experts at the appropriate system commands (SYSCOMs)**

- **Delay Milestone B to program preliminary design review**

- **As an adjunct to 5000, develop a Web-based global map of acquisition guidance**
  - that is updated regularly
  - that only points to current authoritative directive policy

RAND   *Recommendations consistent with DAPA and 2005 DSB summer study   12

By synthesizing the findings from the DSB and DAPA studies, we can glean a number of recommendations for improving DoD 5000-series guidance and, specifically, how to improve the way in which that guidance relates to high–IT content programs and how this guidance addresses interoperability. While neither the DSB nor DAPA study contains these specific recommendations, these suggested improvements are consistent with the themes established in both studies. The recommendations we outline below pertain to high–IT content programs.

Our first recommendation is that DoD should establish technology readiness levels (TRLs) for key GIG functional areas that are important for interoperability, such as waveform functions, communication protocols, IA functions, quality-of-service (QoS) signaling and protocols, and other areas. New guidance should specify that the GIG TRLs be used in reviews of GIG and GIG-related programs. In addition, new guidance should specify that the TRLs be updated based on the learning acquired in program reviews. Technology changes and matures, so these TRLs should be changed and updated as time goes on; specifying an ongoing updating procedure will help ensure that the TRLs remain relevant and current.

Another important recommendation is to include guidance in the DoD 5000 series that ensures that independent technical experts review system designs, especially those aspects of the design that relate to system interoperability or net-centricity. In some cases in which very specialized technologies are being developed or employed, finding experts may be difficult, so the DoD 5000-series guidance should incorporate a degree of flexibility to accommodate such circumstances, but, at the same time, the guidance should encourage all reasonable efforts to conduct reviews of programs by independent experts. The value of such independent reviews is exemplified by the fact that one major command in the Navy has already adopted an independent review policy, though the DoD 5000 series does not yet include such a requirement or recommendation.

Our third recommendation is that the DoD delay MS B to the program's preliminary design review (PDR). At PDR, the program's system design is generally stable and technological maturity has progressed to enable the specification of attainable cost, schedule, and performance thresholds. This recommendation is consistent with the DAPA findings.

Finally, we recommend that DoD develop a Web-based, global map of acquisition guidance as a supplement to the hard-copy 5000-series documentation. The global map should link the 5000-series guidance with all of the key underlying policy guidance. The material on the Web site should be current and include only authoritative directive policy. Maintaining currency will require that the material on the Web site be updated when any underlying policy is updated. The site should include an interactive capability so that a PM can very quickly search for key policy areas such as interoperability and find all of the current policies that must be satisfied and implemented for that specific policy area.

CHAPTER FOUR

Interoperability Policy

Outline

- JCIDS

- Acquisition

→ - Interoperability

- NCIDs

- IA

- Summary

RAND

In this chapter, we turn our attention to interoperability policy. In the following slides, we present a variety of views of global maps of DoD interoperability-related policy documents. Our intent is to illustrate the relationships of the policy documents by showing the organizations responsible and the areas that the policies cover.

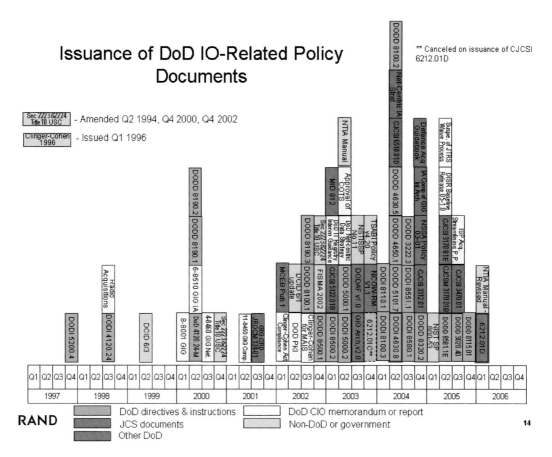

We begin with a slide that shows the multiplicity of DoD policy documents that address interoperability.

A timeline by quarter, starting in 1997 and ending in 2006, is shown at the bottom of the slide. Policy documents related to interoperability are shown in labeled rectangles above the timeline, according the release date of the document. Per the legend on the slide, the colors of the rectangles show the type of document.

This slide shows that there is a dramatic increase in the number of policy documents related to interoperability that have been issued since the first quarter of 2002, with 11 DoD directives and instructions alone in 2004. Clearly, carrying out interoperability policy has required PMs to be aware of many more policy documents in recent years. Furthermore, even if all of the policy documents were consistent and redundant in defining interoperability policy or were, in fact, helpful in providing more detailed guidance on existing policies, the PMs serving since 2002 still have had to comb through a greater volume of literature to ascertain their responsibilities regarding interoperability policy. We will show later that the PM's task is actually more complex because the interoperability policies are neither redundant nor consistent.

Constructing a Global Map of DoD Responsibilities

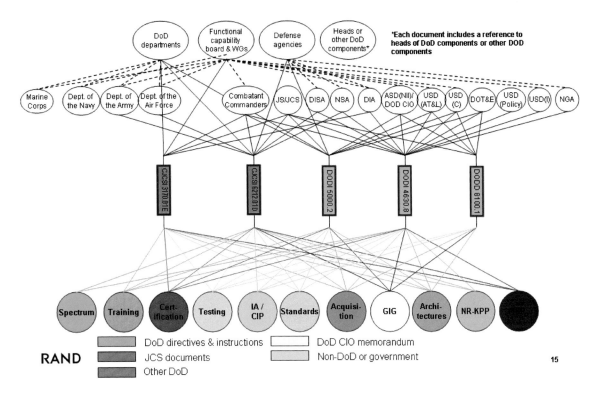

We reviewed the list of interoperability-related policy documents shown in the previous slide to determine which agencies had responsibility for which aspects of interoperability policy. The simplified example in this slide illustrates our analysis methodology.

The row of circles at the bottom shows interoperability-related topic areas that are discussed in one or more of the five policy documents. This list was generated by first reviewing the documents and then synthesizing the collection of areas addressed by the documents. These topic areas are spectrum, training, certification, testing, IA/critical infrastructure protection (CIP), standards, acquisition, GIG, architectures, net-ready key performance parameters (NR-KPPs), and information support plans (ISPs). While the synthesized list does address different aspects of interoperability, the different areas in the list are not necessarily mutually exclusive and were not designed to be. Rather, our intent is to convey the breadth and depth of discussions related to interoperability in the policy documents. Each circle is a different color, and the lines emanating from a particular circle are color-coordinated with the circle so the reader can easily ascertain which topic area is mentioned in the policy documents. A solid line linking a particular topic area to a particular document indicates that that policy document addresses that topic area.

This slide shows a view of five specific documents that either state policies or implement policies: Chairman of the Joint Chiefs of Staff Instruction (CJCSI) 3170.01E (JCS, 2005a), CJCSI 6212.01D (JCS, 2006 [2007]), DoDI 5000.2 (OUSD[AT&L], 2003), DoDI 4630.8 (DoD, 2004g), and DoDD 8100.1 (DoD, 2002c [2003]). These five documents are policy statements or instructions that implement key policies involving interoperability and the GIG. The documents are shown in the five labeled rectangles in the middle of the slide. The colors of the rectangles indicate the type of document and follow the same color-coded legend as in the previous slide.

Organizations that the five policy documents mention by name are shown in the row of circles above the rectangles. Reading from left to right along this second row of labeled circles, the organizations include the military services and various defense agencies and organizations—including the combatant commanders, joint staff (JS), Defense Information Systems Agency (DISA), National Security Agency (NSA), Defense Intelligence Agency (DIA), Assistant Secretary of Defense for Networks and Information Integration (ASD[NII]), DoD chief information officer (CIO), USD(AT&L), USD(C), Defense Office of Testing and Evaluation (DOT&E), USD(Policy), USD(I), and the National Geospatial-Intelligence Agency (NGA). A solid black line linking a document to a specific agency indicates that the policy document assigns, by name, that specific agency to at least one policy responsibility.

The ovals along the top of the diagram show groups of organizations that are tasked with a specific responsibility in at least one of the documents. Therefore, these groups are not the authors of these documents, but they are the entities that, as a result of one of these policy documents, were tasked to execute some action or assume a responsibility. A solid black line linking a policy document to a group of organizations means that the document mentions the group as responsible for a specific policy. Dashed black lines from an oval to circles in the row below the ovals indicate that the specific organization represented by the circle is a member of the group represented by the oval. Therefore, the solid lines connecting the circles, rectangles, and ovals show direct relationships contained in the policy documents. The dashed lines indicate implied relationships. We illustrate these two types of relationships here.

Some of the policy documents do not mention specific organizations but do refer to them as a group. For example, some documents include a global reference such as "Department of Defense departments" or "all defense agencies." The diagram shows these global references with a solid line from the document to the global reference oval, followed by dashed lines from the global reference to the specific entities that are members of that particular global group. It is important to note that this view of DoD responsibilities does not necessarily show all members of each global group. It shows only organizations that are specifically named at some point in one or more of the five documents. There may be many more specific entities that are members of a global group, and all members of each global group, whether or not the member has been mentioned by name in any policy document, do have the responsibility given to a global group by a policy document.

DoDI 5000.2 (OUSD[AT&L], 2003) is an example that illustrates this type of implied responsibility. DoDI 5000.2 does not name NSA, DIA, or the Defense Advanced Research Projects Agency (DARPA) as the specific entities that hold particular responsibilities, but the document does include statements that hold all of the defense agencies accountable for particular responsibilities. To illustrate this global, implied assignment of responsibility, the slide shows a solid line from DoDI 5000.2 to the "Defense agencies" oval on the top row. Dashed lines are shown connecting the "Defense agencies" oval to the specific organizations in the circles on the second row that are defense agencies, including NSA and DIA. The diagram does not show DARPA as a defense agency because none of the five policy documents specifically mentions DARPA. There is, of course, then, no dashed line that connects the "Defense agencies" oval with a "DARPA" circle. DARPA, however, will still be accountable for the responsibilities that DoDI 5000.2 assigns to all defense agencies.

All of the documents contain some general discussion of responsibilities that apply to the heads of DoD components or to other DoD components. *DoD components* refers to all DoD agencies and the military services. Therefore, in this way, the five documents have some reference of generic responsibilities for heads of DoD components and other DoD components. The slide shows the presence of these general discussions with the notation adjacent to the "Heads or other DoD components" oval.

Global Map of DoD Interoperability-Related Policy Documents

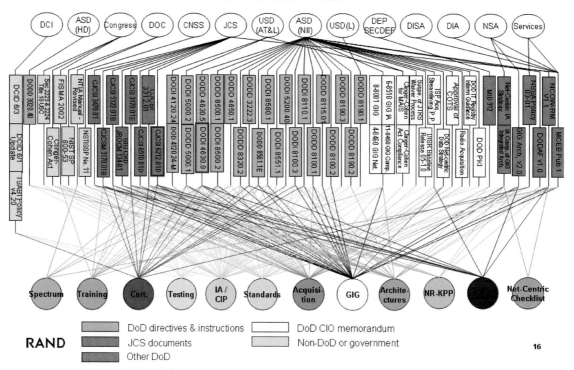

This slide shows a more complete picture of DoD interoperability-related policy documents. In this view, the circles along the bottom show the interoperability-related areas that are addressed by one or more of the policy documents shown in the rectangles in the middle of the diagram. This list of topic areas was generated in the same manner as described in the previous slide, by reviewing the documents and synthesizing the collections of topic areas addressed by the documents. These topic areas are spectrum, training, certification, testing, IA/CIP, standards, acquisition, GIG, architectures, NR-KPPs, ISPs, and net-centric checklists. As in the previous slide, this list of topic areas is meant to convey the breadth and depth of the discussions related to interoperability in the policy documents.

The collection of interoperability-related policy documents included in our analysis is shown in the rectangles in the center of the slide. We generated this collection of policy documents by starting with key interoperability documents, including DoDI 4630.8 (DoD, 2004g) and CJCSI 6212.01D (JCS, 2006 [2007]). We built the collection by reviewing all of the interoperability documents mentioned in the initial set of documents and supplemented that list with other publications identified by DoD. The final collection is shown in the aggregation of rectangles in the middle of the diagram and listed in Appendix A. The rectangles representing the interoperability policy documents are colored according to the type of document the rectangle represents using the color scheme shown at the bottom of the slide.

As in the previous slide, the color-coordinated lines from the circles in the bottom row to the document rectangles in the center indicate that the linked documents address the topic areas named in the circles.

In this view, the ovals at the top of the slide represent the primary authors of the documents. A solid black line from an oval to a document indicates that the organization named in the oval is a primary author of the linked document. Some policy documents show multiple authors, but most show only one organization as the author.

While this particular overview of DoD interoperability-related policy documents may not be optimal for tracing the origins and content of a particular document, this overview does show by the large number of links emanating from ASD(NII) to the collection of policy documents that this organization (and its predecessor, Assistant Secretary of Defense for Command, Control, Communication, and Intelligence [ASD(C3I)] has generated the most policy statements regarding interoperability. Likewise, the JCS have issued many interoperability-related policies. The documents that address the widest range of interoperability topic areas can be identified by observing the bottom portion of this overview. Since DoDI 4630.8 and CJCSI 6212.01D have the most lines linking them to topic areas, it is evident that these two documents address the most topic areas and thus are policy documents central to interoperability. This fact, plus the observation that both DoDI 4360.8 and CJCSI 6212.01D contain interoperability policy statements that address 11 of the 12 topic areas shown in circles at the bottom of the slide (spectrum, training, certification, testing, IA/CIP, standards, acquisition, GIG, architectures, NR-KPPs, and ISPs), identify these documents as prime candidates for review in our quest to uncover inconsistencies and redundancies.

In addition, by observing the number of lines emanating from each topic area along the bottom row of circles, one can identify the topic areas addressed by the largest number of policy documents. This observation is useful because it gives an initial set of areas and documents that contain potential conflicts in policy consistency and redundancy. In this case, topics such as testing, IA/CIP, standards, acquisition, GIG, and (to a slightly lesser extent) architectures are the most-linked topic areas.

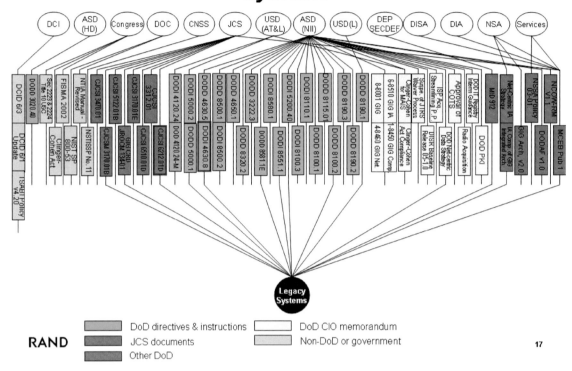

Using a presentation scheme similar to that of the last slide, this slide shows a single topic area in the circle at the bottom—legacy systems. The policy documents are indicated by colored rectangles in the center of the slide. The colors follow the scheme of previous slides as indicated at the bottom of the figure. The ovals at the top of the chart show the agencies that are the principal authors of the documents. A line from an oval to a document indicates that the agency named in the oval is a principal author of the linked document. Lines emanating from the "Legacy Systems" circle at the bottom of the slide to documents in the center rectangles indicate that the linked documents include policy statements about how DoD addresses legacy systems. Policies that address legacy systems are indicated separately from other topics in the previous slide because legacy systems have been a significant source of interoperability problems. We can see that CJCSM 3170.01B (JCS, 2005b); GIG capstone requirements document (CRD) Joint Requirements Oversight Council Memorandum (JROCM) 134-01 (DoD, 2001); CJCSI 6212.01D (JCS, 2006 [2007]); DoDD 8581.1E (DoD, 2005a); DoDI 8551.1 (DoD, 2004j); DoDI 5200.40 (DoD, 1997); DoDD 8100.2 (DoD, 2004d); DoDD 8190.1 (DoD, 2000); "DoD Net-Centric Data Strategy" (DoD CIO, 2003); *Joint Battle Management Command and Control* (DoD, 2003a); "End-to-End IA Component of the GIG Integrated Architecture" (DoD, 2006c); and Military Communications-Electronics Board (MCEB) publication 1 (MCEB, 2002) all contain policies regarding legacy systems.

Significant Overlap Exists Between DoDI 4630.8 and CJCSI 6212.01D

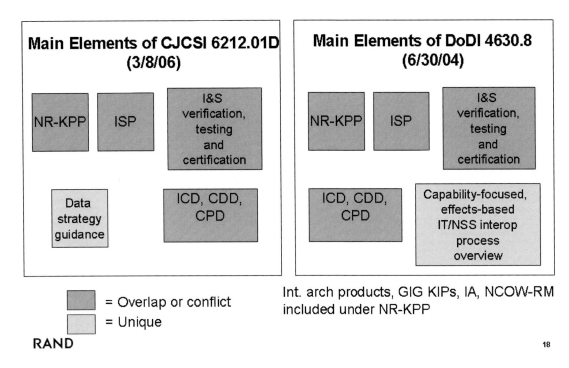

Main Elements of CJCSI 6212.01D (3/8/06)

NR-KPP | ISP | I&S verification, testing and certification

Data strategy guidance | ICD, CDD, CPD

Main Elements of DoDI 4630.8 (6/30/04)

NR-KPP | ISP | I&S verification, testing and certification

ICD, CDD, CPD | Capability-focused, effects-based IT/NSS interop process overview

■ = Overlap or conflict
□ = Unique

Int. arch products, GIG KIPs, IA, NCOW-RM included under NR-KPP

RAND   18

Of the many policy documents on the preceding charts, the two overarching documents are DoD instruction 4630.8 (DoD, 2004g), issued in June 2004, and CJCSI 6212.01D (JCS, 2006 [2007]), issued in March 2006. Though both documents have the same name, the DoD instruction is intended to provide technical requirement guidance, while the Joint Staff instruction is intended to provide interoperability and supportability certification requirement guidance.

There is a high degree of overlap in what these two documents cover, though what is covered in each of the areas is not necessarily consistent. Areas of overlap include the NR-KPP, the ISP, verification testing and certification for interoperability and supportability, and the ICD, CDD, and CPD. The area of data strategy guidance is unique to CJCSI 6212.01D, and the area of capability-focused effects–based IT/National Security Systems (NSS) interoperability process overview is unique to DoDI 4630.8.

Having Separate, Unsynchronized Documents Results in Conflicting Guidance

	CJCSI 6212.01D	DODI 4630.8	ASD(NII) Memo
ISP Process	Addresses tailored ISP (TISP).	Establishes baseline ISP process	Establishes & encourages alternative process (ISP Pilot Program)
ISP Waiver	Addressed for TISP	Waived if JCIDS documentation waived. Request waiver by memo	If JCIDS document waived or JCIDS or JS analysis shows NR-KPP not needed, request waiver by email
Int. Architecture Products for NR-KPP	Requirement includes OV-7, SV-2, SV-11, TV-2	Does not require OV-7, SV-2, SV-11, TV-2	NA
Criterion for interface to be key interface	Includes: •Very large number of point-to-point interfaces •Large number of providers or consumers	Does not include: •Very large number of point-to-point interfaces •Large number of providers or consumers	NA
Required as part of KIP	Refined OV and SV products, TV-1 and TV-SV bridge, TV-2, procedures for testing	Refined OV and SV products, ICD/spec, engineering mgmt plan, CM plan, TV-1 and TV-SV bridge, procedures for testing	NA

RAND   19

In this slide, we compare the guidance offered in CJCSI 6212.01D (JCS, 2006 [2007]), DoDI 4630.8 (DoD, 2004g), and an ASD(NII) memorandum (ASD[NII], 2005b).

With regard to the ISP process, there are not only differences between CJCSI 6212.01D (JCS, 2006 [2007]) and DoDI 4630.8 (DoD, 2004g), but also differences between each of those documents and the 2005 ASD(NII) memo (ASD[NII], 2005b), the subject of which was ISP acquisition streamlining pilot program. CJCSI 6212.01D addresses tailored ISP (TISP), while DoDI 4630.8 establishes a baseline ISP process, and the ASD(NII) memorandum establishes and encourages an alternative process called the ISP pilot program. Some of the differences are in the ISP process itself. The baseline process for the ISP was set forth in DoDI 4630.8. That process was significantly streamlined within the ISP alternative pilot program in the ASD(NII) memorandum. Not only did the alternative pilot program involve significant streamlining, but the use of that alternative was also strongly encouraged in the ASD memorandum. One subset of that memorandum addressed a TISP applicable to acquisition category (ACAT) II and below and non-ACAT programs.[1] It is only that TISP that is addressed in CJCSI 6212.01D, not the remainder of the streamlined program. Clearly, a PM who was not familiar with the details of each policy would be at risk of violating at least one of them. At the same time, even if PMs were aware of all three, simultaneous compliance with the intent of all three policies would be challenging at best. Further complicating the issue is that there is no guidance stipulating when one policy rather than another should be followed.

---

[1] See DoD (2006b) for more details.

Turning to the area of integrated architectures, we find that there are significant differences between CJCSI 6212.01D (JCS, 2006 [2007]) and DoDI 4630.8 (DoD, 2004g) regarding what integrated architecture products are needed for the NR-KPP, what the criteria are for an interface to be specified as a key interface, and what is required as part of a key interface profile (KIP). First, in CJCSI 6212.01D, the requirements for integrated architecture products for the NR-KPP include an operational-view (OV)–7 (logical data model), system-view (SV)–2 (system communication description), SV-11 (physical schema), and technical standards–view (TV)–2 (technical standards forecast). None of these is required in DoDI 4630.8. Second, in CJCSI 6212.01D, the specifications of criteria for an interface to be considered a key interface include (1) whether the interface has a very large number of point-to-point interfaces and (2) whether the interface includes a large number of providers or consumers. These criteria are not included as conditions for designation as a key interface in DoDI 4630.8. Third, CJCSI 6212.01D requires that, as part of a KIP, an OV and SV product be included and that TV-1, TV-SV bridge, and the TV-2 and procedures for testing be included. In DoDI 4630.8, the refined OV and SV products are again included, but there are also requirements for an ICD or specification for the engineering management plan; configuration management plan; and, again, as in CJCSI 6212.01D, the TV-1 and TV-SV bridge. Procedures for testing are included as a requirement in DoDI 4630.8, as they are in CJCSI 6212.01D. These three detailed examples show that, in the integrated architecture area, a PM is again challenged to comply with all of the stated policies, and, again, no guidance is provided to indicate which policies take precedence over others when all cannot be satisfied.

Payoff for Combining Guidance Is Significant, but Implementing It Will Pose Challenges

Advantages	Disadvantages
•Improved policy consistency •Reduced volume of guidance PMs have to review •Single review for combined document will lead to higher-quality policy •More effective management of programs (requirements and acquisition)	•Current division reflects division of responsibilities and authorities between JCS and ASD(NII) •Combining management process will be a challenge

RAND

20

We anticipate that significant payoffs will accrue from combining the CJCSI 6212.01D (JCS, 2006 [2007]) and DoDI 4630.8 (DoD, 2004g) guidance into a single, coordinated guidance document but realize that these advantages will also generate two significant challenges. Advantages that we anticipate would be first, and perhaps foremost, improved consistency between policies through the elimination of some of the discrepancies that we illustrated in the preceding slide. We anticipate that a single review for a combined document would lead to a more focused and in-depth review that would ultimately lead to a higher-quality policy guidance document. Finally, a combination of the two guidance documents should lead to more effective management of programs by combining under one cover the requirement perspective of CJCSI documentation and the acquisition perspective of ASD(NII) documentation.

At the same time, we recognize that there are potential disadvantages and challenges to combining the policy guidance. Certainly, a management challenge could be created if the two policies were combined. The current arrangement reflects the division of responsibilities and authorities that exists between the JCS and ASD(NII). The combination of policy documents could be accompanied by the merger of existing management and oversight processes into a single process. However, this does not necessarily have to be the case, and we do not recommend this alternative here. If a unified process were created, it would be a challenge to accurately reflect and respect the current division of responsibilities between the JCS and ASD(NII) in a single process.

Summary - DoD Interoperability and Supportability Policy Guidance

- **Findings**
  - Large number of policies place a heavy burden on the PM
  - Interoperability policy issuance increased dramatically in past few years
  - Key guidance documents have been updated separately and contain significant overlap and conflicts in multiple areas
  - Key elements for policy compliance missing: joint architectures
  - Limited availability of GIG-KIPs
    - Needed for NR-KPP
  - Metrics for NR-KPP not developed / specified
    - Needed for development of TEMPs
    - Required to pass Milestone C

- **Recommendations**
  - Combine DoDI 4630.8 and CJCSI 6212.01D into a single overarching DoD interoperability policy document
  - Develop quantitative metrics for NR-KPP, based on essential GIG functions (as defined in the NCIDs)
  - Develop GIG-KPPs based on essential GIG functions (as defined in the NCIDs

RAND

21

In summary, we have found that there is a large number of policy documents, with that number increasing dramatically in recent years. The need to be familiar with all of these documents places a heavy burden on PMs. Key documents have been updated separately without coordination, and this has resulted in a situation in which there are significant overlaps, inconsistencies, and conflicts among policies contained in the documents.

Several elements needed for policy compliance are either missing or limited in availability. These include joint architectures and GIG KIPs, both of which are needed for the NR-KPP, as well as metrics for the NR-KPP that are needed for both the development of test and evaluation master plans (TEMPs) and are required to pass MS C.

Our primary recommendation is that DoDI 4630.8 (DoD, 2004g) and CJCSI 6212.01D (JCS, 2006 [2007]) be combined into a single, overarching, DoD interoperability policy document. We also recommend development of quantitative metrics for the NR-KPP, based on essential GIG functions as established and defined in NCIDs documentation. Similarly, we recommend development of GIG KPPs, again based on essential GIG functions as established and defined in the NCIDs documents. We envision the GIG KPPs as applying initially to core GIG programs and eventually to systems that must interconnect to these key systems when the full functionality of the GIG core becomes available.

We recognize that achieving these recommendations will be challenging, but the advantage of having consistent interoperability policy that is easily accessible and clear will result in more efficient program management and, ultimately, more efficiently developed and effective systems.

Outline

- JCIDS

- Acquisition

- Interoperability

 - NCIDs

- IA

- Summary

RAND

22

We now turn our attention to a new element of DoD interoperability policy that specifically addresses GIG component system integration and interoperability policy issues: the NCIDs.

NCIDs Requirement Framework

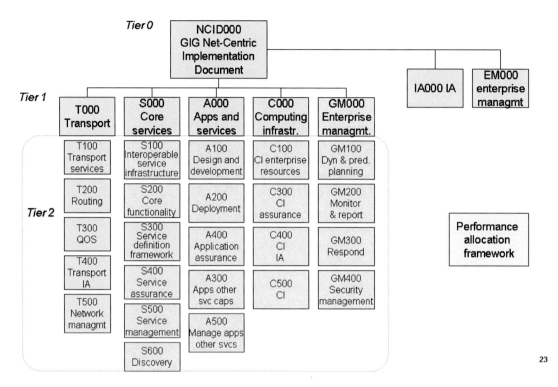

This slide shows the NCID requirement framework contained in the draft version 2 of the NCIDs. The framework has three tiers, with the NCID000 GIG NCID serving as the over-arching policy statement.

The NCIDs are the product of several working groups (WGs) of the GIG E2E system engineering (SE) activity. These DoD-wide working groups were designed to have representation from services, agencies, GIG-related acquisition programs, the Office of the Secretary of Defense, the JCS, and the intelligence community, although some working groups did not have representatives from some DoD organizations.

The objective of the NCIDs are to provide the minimum set of functional performance requirements necessary for users' applications to work effectively in an E2E fashion across the GIG. These requirement documents cover all necessary functional components of the GIG: transport, applications, IA, computing, and services.

Another key element of the NCIDs is the performance allocation (PA) framework, which is discussed later in this chapter.

NCIDs – Purpose and Scope

- **Purpose**
  - **Enterprisewide implementation guidance on system interactions across the GIG**
  - **Specify GIG segment functions necessary to achieve desired end-to-end performance**

- **Provides more detailed design guidance than high-level architecture products (e.g., NCOW reference model)**

- **Scope**
  - **Entire GIG SoS, but initially focused on core GIG programs**

- **Once approved NCIDs to become mandatory parts of the DISR**
  - **All future GIG programs**
  - **All current programs of record that are pre-milestone B within 60 days of April 25, 2005**
  - **Legacy programs not classified "end of life" to develop modification plan to reach compliance or submit request for waiver based on cost, schedule, or performance impact**

RAND   24

The purpose of the NCID is to establish enterprisewide implementation guidance on system interactions across the GIG by specifying GIG segment functions necessary to achieve desired E2E performance. NCIDs provide more detailed design guidance than do high-level architecture products such as the net-centric operations and warfare (NCOW) reference model. NCIDs will eventually address the entire GIG system of systems, but, initially, NCIDs will focus on the core GIG programs. The NCID framework has not yet been approved, but, once it attains approval status, NCIDs will become mandatory parts of the Defense Information Standards Registry (DISR).

As such, when they are approved, it is envisioned that NCIDs will apply to all future GIG programs, all current programs of record that were pre–MS B on June 24, 2005, and all legacy programs not categorized as "end of life." Legacy programs that are not categorized as "end of life" will be required to develop modification plans to reach compliance with the NCID framework or submit a waiver based on disadvantageous cost, schedule, or performance impacts imposed by NCID compliance.

Technology Standards in the NCIDS Are Evolving, Making It Difficult to Provide Meaningful Guidance to PMs

- **Some implied NCID requirements rely on nonexistent standards**
  - PMs are to comply with applicable DoD-approved data models – very few exist
  - QoS signaling (most implementations are proprietary today)

- **Challenge is to be specific to enable interoperability and broad to leave room for important new technologies and solutions**
  - "Chicken or egg" issue for emerging technologies
  - In many areas commercial industry leads in tech development, and standards are proprietary
  - Suggested standards do not provide sufficient guidance to PMs

- **Assumes applications will be services on high-speed IP networks – not accurate for all tactical users for many years**

- **Unclear as to what GIG core services will deliver and what PMs will need to provide**
  - *GIG boundary not well defined*

RAND   25

The technology standards in the NCIDs are currently evolving. This implies that NCIDs, at least in some cases, cannot currently provide meaningful and specific guidance to PMs on which technical approaches or standards they should follow. Furthermore, some implied NCID requirements rely on standards that are not specified. PMs are required by NCIDs to comply with applicable DoD-approved data models, but very few data models exist. The current NCID requirement framework does not even explicitly include data as a segment. In addition, some implementations of higher-level GIG functions, such as QoS signaling, exist, but many implementations are currently proprietary. This can make unified compliance with a universal GIG QoS standard very difficult to achieve in a multivendor network such as the GIG.

The evolution of the NCIDs is governed by two principles that can pose conflicting challenges. First, NCIDs must be specific enough to enable interoperability. Second, and at the same time, NCIDs must be broad enough to allow for incorporation of important new technologies and solutions. This situation creates a chicken-or-egg-first issue for emerging technologies. Further complicating the picture are the facts that, in many areas, commercial industry leads in technology development and that the standards that commercial industry develops are frequently proprietary and may not easily adapt to widespread use across the GIG. In addition, the current NCID guidance is not time phased, and the performance assessment framework is not tied explicitly to operational and system architectures. Because of these issues, the standards currently contained in the NCIDs (i.e., draft version 2 of the NCIDs) do not provide sufficient guidance to PMs to achieve interoperability.[1]

Therefore, the current NCID requires further development before it can be considered workable guidance. At a minimum, some assumptions need to be closely examined for accuracy, and a more detailed definition of GIG core services should be provided. For example, in its current state, the NCID framework assumes that applications will be services with high-speed, internet protocol (IP)–based networks. This assumption will not be generally accurate for all tactical users and especially not for tactical users on the move. The current NCID is also unclear about what GIG core services will deliver and what PMs will need to provide. Without clear and specific definition of where GIG core enterprise service functionality and reach end and where local program services being developed by tactical PMs begin, PMs will have insufficient guidance on how to design systems that will be interoperable with the GIG.

---

[1] In this case, RAND's findings have been confirmed by comments forwarded to RDA CHSENG by some Navy PMs.

Estimating E2E GIG System Performance: NCID Performance Allocation Across Segments

- GIG segments to be interoperable
  - in accordance with approved requirements documents
  - will also adhere to PAs defined by NCIDs

- PA framework will provide overall PA specifications
  - PA specifications will be used by ASD(NII) GIG SE to assess E2E performance of the GIG in specific mission areas

- Findings
  - Most version 2.0 NCIDs did not include PA specifications, to be included in 3.0
  - Improved net-centric IER data sets and server architectures needed
    - Data centers, DNS, BFT/COP/UDOP data streaming
    - Appropriate JCIDS CBA results
  - Additional high-level simulation tools may be needed to assess network performance and scalability
  - GIG TEN NCIDs will be key for many PMs

RAND   26

The NCIDs address PA across segments, stipulating that GIG segments be interoperable in accordance with approved requirement documents. The GIG segments will also be required to adhere to PAs defined by NCIDs. The PA framework will provide overall PA specifications. These PA specifications will be used by the ASD(NII) GIG SE to assess E2E performance of the GIG in specific mission areas.

Our review of the version 2.0 NCIDs shows that most of the documents did not include PA specifications, but these are expected to be included in version 3.0 NCIDs. We also found that improved net-centric information exchange requirement (IER) data sets and server architectures will be needed, particularly for data centers, domain name services (DNSs), and blue force tracking (BFT), and for common operational picture (COP) and user-defined operational picture (UDOP) data streaming. Results of appropriate JCIDS CBAs could be used. We also found that additional, high-level simulation tools may be needed to assess network performance and scalability. Finally, we believe that the GIG tactical edge network (TEN) NCIDs will be a key policy resource for many PMs.

CHAPTER SIX

Information Assurance Policy

Outline

- JCIDS
- Acquisition
- Interoperability
- NCIDs

 - IA

- Summary

RAND   27

We now turn our attention to IA. We uncovered 38 documents that contain policy statements that address IA. The review of all 38 is discussed in this chapter.

Global Map of DoD IA-Related Policy Documents

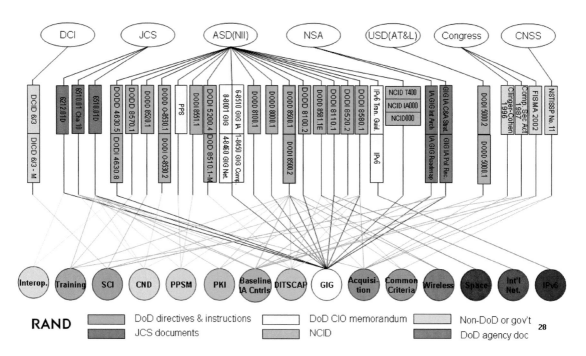

Using the same structure we employed earlier to view policy documentation relating to interoperability, this slide shows a mapping of DoD IA-related policy documents to their respective authors and the different IA topic areas that the policies in the documentation cover.

In this slide, the ovals along the top row represent the entity author of the IA document. These entity authors include the Director of Central Intelligence (DCI), JCS, ASD(NII), NSA, USD(AT&L), Congress, and the Committee on National Security Systems (CNSS). The documents represented by colored rectangles in the middle of the slide are the DoD policy documents and other government policy documents related to the issue of IA. The color of the rectangle associated with each document indicates the type of document per the legend shown at the bottom of the slide. A solid black line between an oval and a rectangle indicates that the entity named in the oval is a primary author of the document represented by the rectangle.

The circles near the bottom of the slide are the IA topic areas addressed by the policy documents. These topic areas are interoperability; training; secret compartmentalized information (SCI); computer network defense (CND); port, protocol, and service management (PPSM); public key infrastructure (PKI); baseline of IA controls; the DITSCAP process; GIG; and acquisition, common criteria, wireless, space, international networks, and IPv6. The slide shows each topic area in a different color, and color-coordinated lines emanating between a circle and a document indicate that the document addresses the linked topic area in its policy statements.

This overview diagram shows that most of the policies relating to IA are authored by ASD(NII) (and its predecessor, ASD[C3I]). By observing the number of lines between each circled topic area and the rectangles, one can conclude that many policy documents address topic areas such as baseline IA controls, the DITSCAP process, the GIG, and acquisition. The GIG is the most highly impacted area, with 13 documents addressing GIG policy. Similarly, by observing the number of lines emanating from each document rectangle, one can conclude that the policy documents that address the most IA topic areas are DoDD 8500.1 (DoD, 2002d) and DoDI 8500.2 (DoD, 2003b). These two documents are outlined in red to indicate that they are key IA policies.

Issuance of DoD IA-Related Policy Documents

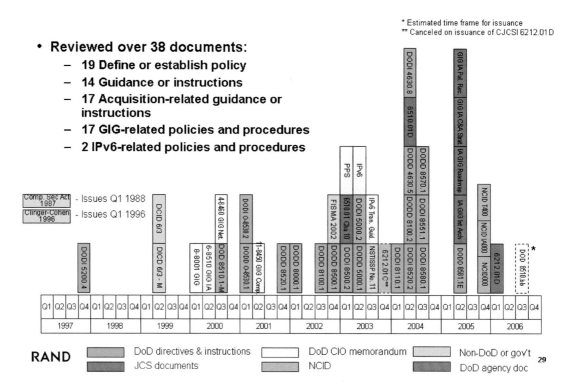

This slide shows the currency and multiplicity of DoD policy documents that address IA.

A timeline by quarter, starting in 1997 and ending in 2006, is shown at the bottom of the slide. Policy documents related to IA are shown in labeled rectangles above the timeline according the release date of the document. The type of document is also shown by the colors of the rectangles. Green indicates that the document is a DoD directive or instruction. Magenta represents JCS documents. Yellow represents a DoD CIO memorandum. Purple indicates NCIDs. Gold indicates a non-DoD government document. Finally, orange indicates a DoD agency document. Note that this color scheme differs from the one presented earlier for interoperability documents.

This slide shows that there is a dramatic increase in the number of policy documents related to IA that have been issued since the first quarter of 2003, with nine policy statements issued in 2003, followed by another nine in 2004, and eight more in 2005. The timeline shows some promise of a decreased rate in 2006 or 2007. For example, this timeline shows only one new policy document for IA and information security certifications being issued in 2006, DoDI 8510.bb, *Defense Information Assurance Certification Accreditation Program (DIACAP)* (DoD, 2006a). However, there are reasons to believe that IA policy issuance will again increase after DIACAP is implemented.

Challenges of Applying DoD IA Policies to DoD Information Systems

- **Large number of IA policy documents**
  - **Did not find significant inconsistencies in DoD IA policy**
  - **Identified some inconsistencies with DoD and Navy IA policies**
  - **New policy now in effect: DoDI 8510.bb DIACAP**

- **DIACAP 8510.bb released as interim guidance in July 2006, a significant number of documents will have to be updated to maintain consistency**

- **8500 Series includes exemptions for embedded systems and platform IT not connected to the GIG, but an increasing number of exempted systems will be connected in real time to the GIG, including**
  - **weapon systems** → **UAVs/UGVs**
  - **voice communications** → **voice over IP**
  - **embedded systems** → **radar (e.g., Navy CEC)**

- **Should a universal IA policy be created and applied to all DoD warfighting systems or development of separate IA policies for previously exempted systems?**

- **Changes in the information infrastructure are making new demands on IA**
  - **Traditional enclave and system boundaries are breaking down**

RAND   30

This slide summarizes the major findings regarding DoD IA policy.

As shown in the previous slide, a large number of different policies and continuing policies is being issued by DoD, the military services, and DoD agencies concerning IA. This fact makes it difficult to keep this body of policy statements synchronized and up to date. However, as opposed to the case with interoperability, the body of DoD IA policy appears to be internally consistent. Our review reveals only some minor inconsistencies between DoD IA policies and Navy IA policies.[1]

A major update to DoD IA policy, DoDI 8510.bb (DoD, 2006a) was released as interim guidance in July 2006. DIACAP replaces DITSCAP. The IA topic-area chart presented earlier shows that seven other IA documents address DITSCAP, so those seven documents and possibly others will have to be updated to maintain the internal DoD IA policy consistency with the new DIACAP policy.

---

[1] It should be noted that only minor inconsistencies between DoD and Department of the Navy IA policies were identified. Specifically, DoD instruction 5200.40 (DoD, 1997, §2.3) states that certification and accreditation (C&A) applies to any IT system, while SECNAV instruction 5239.3A (SECNAV, 2004, p. 12, §7.e) states that C&A is required only for systems that are connected to GIG. In addition, DoD directive 8500.1 (DoD, 2002d, p. 2, §§2.1.2.1, 2.1.2.6) and DoD instruction 5200.40 state that the scope of the IA policies would cover all NSS IT systems "including Special Access Program" and "stand alone information systems." SECNAV 5239.3A (p. 5, §5.b) states that its policies will not superscede DCI policies regarding SCI or special access programs. Finally, DoD instruction 5200.40 (p. 14, §E3.3.3.4) defines the user representative as the liaison for the user community to the DITSCAP process. Neither OPNAV instruction 5239.1B (OPNAV, 1999) nor SECNAV instruction 5239.3A provides guidance for identifying a user representative for the DITSCAP process.

Another important finding that was discovered during this investigation was the challenges associated with the exceptions built into the DoD 8500-series documents. These exceptions exclude certain types of IT systems from the requirements for IA. These exceptions include information technologies embedded into systems such as weapon platforms as well as information technologies that were considered not to be in any way connected to the GIG. However, we are seeing over time that new technologies are being introduced into some systems that were originally exempt and that these new technologies are challenging the preconceived notion of what should be exempt from IA requirements or policy. For example, unmanned aerial vehicles (UAVs) and unmanned ground vehicles (UGVs) in the military forces were originally expected to be exempt from IA requirements. However, UAVs and UGVs in the military forces have evolved, and these platforms are now heavily integrated into networks and into IT, so any exemptions that might allow such systems to escape meeting the same IA requirements need to be revisited.

Similarly, voice communication was originally considered exempt from many of the requirements for IA or information security. Since that decision, we have moved to increasing use of voice over IP in some systems. This development warrants a reinvestigation of the exemption of voice communication from IA requirements.

Even certain embedded systems—such as radar, which used to be considered separate and not part of network communication—now, increasingly, are becoming part of network communication. Applications such as the Navy's cooperative engagement capability (CEC), in which radar information is shared among both aircraft and surface platforms such as Navy ships to provide a more complete picture of radar space, is an example of an embedded system that was originally considered a good case for exemption but that may no longer meet the intent of the DoD 8500-series exceptions.

These examples illustrate that systems that were once considered embedded and isolated to the platform itself are now sharing information throughout the GIG to provide more complete views of the COP in military operations. This means that we need to identify the exemptions that exist for those systems and determine whether the exemptions should still apply if the system is now sharing information over the military networks.

Our analysis of the exemption issue leads to more questions: Should there, in fact, be a universal IA policy that applies to all DoD warfighting IT systems? Is such a universal policy necessary, or is the current policy with synchronization, patches, and updating sufficient to reflect changes in how IT is being used? Which option will best be able to provide adequate policy guidance for providing IA?

Finally, changes in IT and the military's increasing use of IT are creating new demands on current IA policy. The expected increase of GIG tactical networks and the future vision for GIG tactical networks in which there will be communities of interest (COIs) that are created dynamically for members just prior to a mission are examples of areas in which current IA policy may fall short. Other areas include IA policy for the products of sensor and information fusion. The full concept of COIs is still being reviewed, but the use of IPv6 indicates an increasing use of dynamic networks and ad hoc networks. These types of networks create a tremendous strain and challenge for traditional concepts of enclaves and boundaries. Therefore, new policies will need to be developed that will be able to accommodate the dynamic networks that may emerge with thousands of nodes for a single mission.

Another challenge on the horizon comes with the introduction of IPv6. IPv6 will provide a large number of IP addresses, and this provision will potentially allow a single soldier to be equipped with several devices, each of which has its own IP network, its own IP address, and, possibly, different security classifications for each IP address. Therefore, concepts and methods for managing a multiplicity of IP addresses, each with its own set of access and use characteristics, will be have to be developed. The management system developed will have to address how to achieve IA in such future operating environments.

CHAPTER SEVEN

Summary

Outline

- JCIDS

- Acquisition

- Interoperability

- NCIDs

- IA

 - Summary

RAND   31

A summary of our study follows.

Summary – Findings

- **There has been a proliferation of policy documents in recent years and guidance is often not actionable**
  - **policy issuance has sharply increased in the past few years**
  - **we found conflicts and overlaps in interoperability policy**

- **GIG guidance and standards are still evolving and not yet "stable"**
  - **rapid technology change**
  - **PA framework under development**
  - **key technologies being developed under the leadership of commercial industry**

- **Large number of IA policies**
  - **many will have to be updated to be consistent with DoDI 8510.bb, which is now in effect**

RAND

32

In this briefing, we have examined a broad set of DoD IT- and interoperability-related policies. We found that policy issuance has increased sharply in recent years. By mapping the policies to key areas and examining the details, we found that some conflicts and redundancies exist among the collection of policies included in our study. Most of these conflicts are in the area of interoperability policy. The conflicts and redundancies contribute to the inactionable nature of some of the policies.

We found GIG guidance and standards to be imprecise from a technical standpoint and still evolving. The changes are being fueled by rapid changes in technology. In addition, DoD standards development is difficult because industry leadership in standards development imparts a proprietary nature on some resulting standards.

Summary – Recommendations

- **Streamline DoD IT policy and make it more actionable by PMs**
  - **Reduce number of interoperability and IA policies**
  - **GIG TEN NCIDs will be key for many PMs**

- **In JCIDS, improve requirements traceability from COCOM needs statements to program development documents**

- **For interoperability, DoD should combine CJCSI 6212.01D and DoDI 4630**
  - **Develop under the joint leadership of ASD(NII) and J6**

- **Acquisition**
  - **Establish technology risk areas and TRLs for GIG interoperability areas**
  - **Ensure independent tech assessment of GIG program interoperability approaches by appropriate SYSCOMs or DISA**
  - **Move Milestone B to PDR, at least for high–IT content programs**

- **In version 3.0 NCIDs**
  - **Clearly define GIG core services, which programs will provide them, needed network bandwidth – to reduce potential duplication of effort**
  - **Reduce reliance on proprietary standards for functions that must cross segment boundaries – QoS signaling**
  - **Service operational communities should review GIG use cases to be used in the PA framework**

RAND   33

Our examination of DoD IT-related policy leads to several recommendations. First, we recommend that DoD IT-related policy be streamlined by reducing the number of policies in specific areas, such as interoperability and IA. This move will allow PMs and other stakeholders to determine which policies apply to their particular programs and what party is responsible for the attendant actions, events, and deliverables. Along this same vein, the policies should be more actionable for PMs. This last point is especially important for the GIG TEN NCIDs, which will be a key policy resource for many DoD managers of tactical programs.

Second, regarding JCIDS, the requirement traceability from COCOM needs statements to program development documents should be improved, especially as these pertain to interoperability requirements. Third, interoperability policy would be improved by combining CJCSI 6212.1D (JCS, 2006 [2007]) with DoDI 4630 (DoD, 2004g) and developing the new combined policy under the joint leadership of ASD(NII) and the command, control, communication, and computer (C4) directorate (J6). Implementation of these first three recommendations would reduce the volume of literature that addresses interoperability and IA policy and make the policy more user oriented.

Fourth, with regard to acquisition, technology risk areas and TRLs for GIG functional areas should be established. In addition, the acquisition policy should ensure independent assessment of technology risk for programs by appropriate SYSCOMs or DISA. High–IT content programs will have a higher probability of meeting cost, schedule, and performance goals if MS B is moved to the current PDR point on the acquisition timeline. Implementing this set of recommendations will result in a better understanding of technology risk and how best to handle it.

We also recommend that version 3.0 NCIDs clearly define GIG core services, identify which programs will provide them, specify the network bandwidth needed to support them, and state what functionality they will provide. This clarification will reduce the potential for duplication of effort by the PMs and will aid in the convergence of interface specifications. Furthermore, version 3.0 NCIDs should reduce the reliance on proprietary standards for functions that must cross segment boundaries, such as QoS signaling. In addition, version 3.0 NCIDs should allow service operational communities not only to review GIG use cases that are to be used in the performance allocation framework, but also to be offered greater opportunity to participate in their development.

Implementation of our recommendations is likely to present a number of challenges, but the potential benefits of implementing these recommendations to DoD IT-related policy far outweigh the obstacles that may have to be overcome otherwise.

Additional Details for Selected Topics

DSB and DAPA Recommendations to Improve Acquisition System Performance

- ## DSB
  - Move from requirement-based to judgment-based execution
    - Force capability trade-offs to maintain cost and schedule
  - Use technical red teams to independently assess tech feasibility
  - Rigorously enforce the TRL process
  - Include integration risk and manufacturing readiness in the technical assessment.

- ## DAPA
  - Shift to time-certain-development - make *schedule* a KPP
    - Require IOC to occur no later than six years after Milestone A
    - Trade off technical performance to achieve schedule
  - Establish TRLs for system design
  - Realign Milestone B to occur at preliminary design review
  - Require program TEMPs and initial OT&E plans to be completed prior to Milestone B
  - Enhance PM authority so they can defer non-KPP requirements to later program blocks or upgrades

RAND   34

This appendix contains a few additional slides that further illuminate points made in the body of this document.

Our study cited several recommendations from the DSB and DAPA to improve acquisition system performance. The DSB recommended that DoD move from requirement-based to judgment-based execution and make force capability trade-offs to maintain cost and schedule goals. The DSB also recommended that DoD use technical red teams to independently assess technological feasibility and rigorously enforce the TRL process and include integration risk and manufacturing readiness in the technical assessment.

DAPA recommended a shift to time-certain development and making the schedule a key performance parameter (KPP). In addition, it recommended that there be a requirement for initial operational capability (IOC) to occur no later than six years after MS A and that trade-offs in technical performance be made to achieve schedule goals. It also recommended that TRLs be established for system design; that MS B be realigned at PDR; that program TEMPs and initial operational test and evaluation (OT&E) plans be completed to pass MS B; and, finally, that PM authority be enhanced so that PMs can defer non-KPP requirements to later program blocks or upgrades.

DIACAP Provides a New Certification and Accreditation Process

- **DIACAP establishes new procedures for authorizing the operation of DoD information systems (ISs)**
    - **Will replace DoD 5200.40 (DoD, 1999) (DITSCAP) and DoD 6-8510 (DoD CIO, 2000a) (DITSCAP manual)**
    - **Comply with DoDI 8500.2 (DoD, 2003b), legislative (FISMA), and IC (DCID 6/1) (Director of Central Intelligence, 1995 [2003]) policies.**
    - **Shift from individual systems to enterprise perspective consistent with the GIG**
- **IA controls based on mission assurance category (MAC) and confidentiality level (CL)**
- **Responsibility for establishing, managing, and tracking the status of DoD IS within the DIACAP rests with the DoD component IA programs***
- **DIACAP includes online portal and Web tools for supporting DIACAP execution**
- **Findings:**
    - **Reaccreditation every year instead of every three years**
    - **All ISs inherit enterprise IA standards and requirements as baseline requirements; however**
        - **Certification and accreditation is still structured on a per-system basis**
        - **System IA controls can be augmented to address local threats or vulnerabilities**
        - **CA process suited for static environments; not well suited for dynamic COIs**
        - **What defines the "enterprise"? Who defines the enterprise IA baseline controls?**

RAND   *Staten (2005)
           **Wierum (2005); Bendel (2006)   36

This slide outlines the new certification and accreditation process that DIACAP will provide. The roles and responsibilities for IA certification and approval to operate for the system under development are summarized below. The key IA certification authority is the **designated approval authority (DAA)**.

The DAA has the authority and ability to evaluate the mission, business cases, and budgetary needs for the system in view of the security risks. The DAA determines the acceptable level of residual risk and makes the authorization decision, and it is ultimately responsible for authorizing or denying the test or operation of DoD ISs (DoD CIO, 2007, paragraph 5.14.5).

Also, DoD CIO (2007, paragraph 5.14.2) recognizes that the DAA is responsible for ensuring that each DoD IS complies with applicable DoD baseline IA Controls to interconnect with the GIG.

The **IA manager (IAM) (also known as the IS security manager [ISSM])** is responsible for the IA program of a DoD IS or organization.

The **certification authority (CA)** manages the certification process. The IAM or CA performs a comprehensive evaluation of the technical and nontechnical aspects of the certification effort, reports the status of the certification, and recommends to the DAA whether to authorize the system.

The **PM or system manager (SM)** represents the interest of the system throughout the life cycle and assigns an IAM.

The **user representative** is concerned with system availability, integrity, and confidentiality as they relate to the system's mission.

Implications of Internet Protocol version 6 (IPv6) for DoD IA Policy

- In 2003, DoD stated that, as of October 1, 2003, DoD products and systems will be capable of operation in Internet Protocol version 4 (IPv4) and IPv6 networks and that all DoD networks will use IPv6 by FY 2008.*
    - Provide 3.4×10^{38} IP addresses (or 6.5×10^{23} addresses/m^2 of the earth's surface)
        - Eliminate need for Network Address Translation
    - Integrated IP security will improve security for some functions
    - Improved autoconfiguration for mobile networks

- Findings:
    - IA standards for IPv6 are still evolving
    - Overlay of IPv4 and IPv6 opens new potential security issues
    - Military services will not be able to meet 2008 timeline
    - IPv6-enabled mobile, ad hoc networks will stress concepts of enclaves and IA management
        - Each soldier is an enclave with possibly multiple, different MAC/CL networks

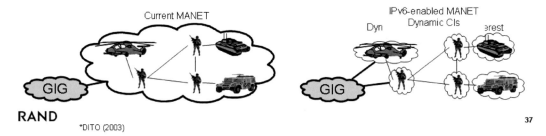

RAND

*DITO (2003)

37

We examined the implications of IPv6 for DoD IA policy. We found that IA standards for IPv6 are still evolving and therefore cannot be fully assessed at this time. It appears, however, that the simultaneous use of IPv4 and IPv6 in the same network could potentially invoke additional security concerns. At this time, there is also considerable uncertainty as to whether the military services will be able to meet the DoD mandate that all DoD networks use IPv6 by FY 2008. One primary issue is that IPv6-enabled, mobile, ad hoc networks could stress the concepts of enclaves and IA management because each soldier could be considered an enclave and each soldier could conceivably be associated with multiple, distinct networks.

Integrated Architectures

- Overarching guidance on selecting and using architectures is insufficient:
    - No definitive list of authoritative architectures
    - No clear authorities for determining which architectures should be used
    - Architectural framework may not be well suited to GIG SOA approach
    - Recommendation: Identify joint and service architectures that should be point of reference for addressing particular mission areas; identify appropriate joint and service authorities that can direct PMs to use particular architectures

- Maintenance and application of architectures are very difficult
    - Architectural-view definitions permit significant variation in what and how information is captured
    - Significant ambiguities are common, especially for data interoperability
    - Architectural-view formats and packages are not compatible with each other
    - Static views are difficult to employ directly, much less integrate, and metrics for assessing integrated architectures are limited
    - Recommendation: Revise architectural-view definitions to provide precise expectations of how products should look based on "best" architectures developed
        - Views should be sufficient to define data interoperability and IA controls
    - Recommendation: Consider developing automated architecture standards and eventually requiring compliance with these standards (e.g., UML 2.0 / SysML)
        - Specifying a common architectural model exchange format would be
    RAND   particularly useful   38

This slide summarizes several issues associated with the definition and development of integrated architectures.

Policy Documents Reviewed

10 U.S. Code 2223, Information Technology: Additional Responsibilities of Chief Information Officers, October 1, 1998.

10 U.S. Code 2224, Defense Information Assurance Program, amended October 30, 2000.

Defense Information Systems Agency, Network Centric Operations and Warfare (NCOW)—Reference Model, July 2, 2003.

———, "Global Information Grid (GIG) Architecture, Version 2.0," December 2003.

Director, Washington Headquarters Service, U.S. Department of Defense, *Department of Defense Procedures for Management of Information Requirements*, DoD 8910.1-M, June 1998.

Director of Central Intelligence, U.S. Department of Defense, *Director of Central Intelligence Directive: Security Policy for Sensitive Compartmented Information and Security Policy*, DCID 6/1, March 1, 1995, administratively updated November 4, 2003.

Federal Information Security Management Act of 2002, 107th Congress, 2nd Session, House of Representatives bill 3844, March 5, 2002.

Military Communications-Electronics Board, *MCEB Organization, Mission and Functions Manual*, MCEB publication 1, March 1, 2002.

National Security Telecommunications and Information Systems Security Committee, *National Policy Governing the Acquisition of Information Assurance (IA) and IA-Enabled Information Technology (IT) Products*, NSTISSP 11, January 2000, revised June 2003.

Office of the Assistant Secretary of Defense for Networks and Information Integration, U.S. Department of Defense, "Temporary Suspension of the Joint Tactical Radio Systems (JTRS) Waive Process," May 23, 2005.

———, "Information Support Plan (ISP) Acquisition Streamlining Pilot Program," memorandum for secretaries of the military departments, under secretaries of defense, assistant secretaries of defense, general counsel of the Department of Defense, inspector general of the Department of Defense, director of operational test and evaluation, assistants to the secretary of defense, director of administration and management, director of program analysis and evaluation, director of force transformation, directors of the defense agencies, director of the joint staff, and directors of the Department of Defense field activities, Washington, D.C., August 26, 2005.

Office of the Intelligence Community Chief Information Officer, "Top Secret/Sensitive Compartmented Information and Below Interoperability (TSABI) Policy," version 4.20, November 24, 2003.

Office of the Under Secretary of Defense for Acquisition, Technology, and Logistics, *Department of Defense Manual: Defense Standardization Program (DSP) Policies and Procedures*, DoD 4120.24-M, March 2000.

Office of the Under Secretary of Defense for Acquisition, Technology, and Logistics, and the Assistant Secretary of Defense for Command, Control, Communications, and Intelligence, "Clinger-Cohen Act Compliance Policy," memorandum for secretaries of the military departments, chair of the Joint Chiefs of Staff, under secretaries of defense, assistant secretaries of defense, general counsel of the Department of Defense, inspector general of the Department of Defense, and the directors of the defense agencies, March 8, 2002.

————, "Clinger-Cohen Act Compliance Policy for Major Automated Information Systems," memorandum for secretaries of the military departments, chair of the Joint Chiefs of Staff, under secretaries of defense, assistant secretaries of defense, general counsel of the Department of Defense, inspector general of the Department of Defense, and the directors of the defense agencies, June 19, 2002.

Ross, Ron, Stu Katzke, Arnold Johnson, Marianne Swanson, Gary Stoneburner, George Rogers, and Annabelle Lee, *Recommended Security Controls for Federal Information Systems*, Gaithersburg, Md.: National Institute of Standards and Technology, NIST special publication 800-53, February 2005.

U.S. Assistant Secretary of Defense, "Department of Defense (DoD) Public Key Infrastructure (PKI)," memorandum, May 21, 2002.

U.S. Assistant Secretary of Defense for Command, Control, Communications, and Intelligence, "Radio Acquisitions," memorandum, August 28, 1998.

————, *Department of Defense Directive: DoD Logistics Use of Electronic Data Interchange (EDI) Standards*, DoDD 8190.1, May 5, 2000.

————, "Approval of Commercial Off-the-Shelf Information Technology/National Security Systems Software Action Plan," memorandum, April 8, 2003.

U.S. Department of Defense, *Department of Defense Directive: Management and Use of the Radio Frequency Spectrum*, DoDD 4650.1, June 24, 1987.

————, *Department of Defense Instruction: DoD Information Technology Security Certification and Accreditation Process (DITSCAP)*, DoDI 5200.40, December 30, 1997.

————, *Department of Defense Directive: Military Communications-Electronics Board (MCEB)*, DoDD 5100.35, March 10, 1998.

————, *Department of Defense Instruction: Defense Standardization Program (DSP)*, DoDI 4120.24, June 18, 1998, administrative reissuance incorporating change 1, March 9, 2000.

————, *Department of Defense Directive: The Department of Defense (DoD) Electronic Business/Electronic Commerce (EB/EC) Program*, DoDD 8190.2, June 23, 2002.

————, *Department of Defense Directive: Smart Card Technology*, DoDD 8190.3, August 31, 2002.

————, *Department of Defense Directive: Global Information Grid (GIG) Overarching Policy*, DoDD 8100.1, September 19, 2002, certified current through November 21, 2003.

————, *Department of Defense Directive: Information Assurance (IA)*, DoDD 8500.1, October 24, 2002.

————, *Joint Battle Management Command and Control*, MID 912, January 7, 2003.

————, *Department of Defense Instruction: Information Assurance (IA) Implementation*, DoDI 8500.2, February 6, 2003.

————, *Department of Defense Instruction: Operation of the Defense Acquisition System*, DoDI 5000.2, May 12, 2003.

————, *Department of Defense Architecture Framework*, version 1.0, August 30, 2003.

————, *National Security Space Acquisition Policy: Guidance for DoD Space System Acquisition Process*, NSSAP 03-01, October 6, 2003.

————, *Department of Defense Instruction: Department of Defense (DOD) Voice Networks*, DoDI 8100.3, January 16, 2004.

————, *Department of Defense Instruction: Multinational Information Sharing Networks Implementation*, DoDI 8110.1, February 6, 2004.

————, *Department of Defense Directive: Use of Commercial Wireless Devices, Services, and Technologies in the Department of Defense (DoD) Global Information Grid (GIG)*, DoDD 8100.2, April 14, 2004.

————, *Department of Defense Directive: Interoperability and Supportability of Information Technology (IT) and National Security Systems (NSS)*, DoDD 4630.5, May 5, 2004.

————, *Department of Defense Directive: DoD Executive Agent for Information Technology Standards*, DoDD 5101.7, May 21, 2004, certified current as of November 3, 2006.

————, *Department of Defense Instruction: Procedures for Interoperability and Supportability of Information Technology (IT) and National Security Systems (NSS)*, DoDI 4630.8, June 30, 2004.

————, "Net-Centric IA Strategy," June 30, 2004.

————, *Department of Defense Instruction: Information Assurance (IA) in the Defense Acquisition System*, DoDI 8580.1, July 9, 2004.

————, *Department of Defense Instruction: Ports, Protocols, and Services Management (PPSM)*, DoDI 8551.1, August 13, 2004.

————, *Department of Defense Directive: DoD Electromagnetic Environmental Effects (E3) Program*, DoDD 3222.3, September 8, 2004.

————, *Department of Defense Directive: Data Sharing in a Net-Centric Department of Defense*, DoDD 8320.02, December 2, 2004, certified current as of April 23, 2007.

————, *Department of Defense Directive: Information Assurance (IA) Policy for Space Systems Used by the Department of Defense*, DoDD 8581.1E, June 21, 2005.

————, *Department of Defense Directive: Defense Critical Infrastructure Program (DCIP)*, DoDD 3020.40, August 19, 2005.

————, *Department of Defense Directive: Information Technology Portfolio Management*, DoDD 8115.01, October 10, 2005.

————, *Defense Acquisition Guidebook*, Washington, D.C.: U.S. Department of Defense, July 24, 2006.

————, "End-to-End IA Component of the GIG Integrated Architecture," October 26, 2006.

U.S. Department of Defense Chief Information Officer, "Department of Defense Global Information Grid Information Assurance," guidance and policy memorandum 6-8510, June 2000.

————, "GIG Networks," guidance and policy memorandum 4-8460, August 24, 2000.

————, "Global Information Grid (GIG) Computing," guidance and policy memorandum 11-8450, April 6, 2001.

————, "DoD Net-Centric Data Strategy," memorandum for secretaries of the military departments, chair of the Joint Chiefs of Staff, under secretaries of defense, director of defense research and evaluation, assistant secretaries of defense, general counsel of the U.S. Department of Defense, inspector general of the U.S. Department of Defense, director of operational test and evaluation, assistants to the secretary of defense, director of administration and management, director of force transformation, director of net assessment, directors of the defense agencies, and directors of U.S. Department of Defense field activities, May 9, 2003.

U.S. Department of Defense Deputy Chief Information Officer, "Department of Defense Information Technology (IT) Registry Interim Guidance," memorandum, March 17, 2003.

U.S. Department of Defense Information Technology Standards Registry (DISR) baseline release.

U.S. Deputy Secretary of Defense, "DoD Chief Information Officer (CIO) Guidance and Policy Memorandum No. 8-8001—March 31, 2000—Global Information Grid," memorandum for secretaries of the military departments; chair of the Joint Chiefs of Staff; under secretaries of defense; director of defense research and engineering; assistant secretaries of defense; general counsel of the Department of Defense; inspector general of the Department of Defense; director of operational test and evaluation; commanders of the Combatant Command; assistants to the secretary of defense; director of administration and management; directors of the defense agencies; director of the National Reconnaissance Office; directors of Department of Defense field activities; chief information officers of the military departments; director of the joint staff for command, control, communication, and computer systems; chief information officers of the defense agencies; director of the intelligence community management staff; and the intelligence community chief information officer, March 31, 2000.

U.S. Joint Chiefs of Staff, *Chairman of the Joint Chiefs of Staff Instruction: Theater Joint Tactical Networks Configuration Control Board Charter*, CJCSI 5122.01B, August 23, 2001.

———, *Chairman of the Joint Chiefs of Staff Instruction: NAVSTAR Global Positioning System Selective Availability Anti-Spoofing Module Requirements,* CJCSI 6140.01A, March 31, 2004.

———, *Chairman of the Joint Chiefs of Staff Instruction: Information Assurance (IA) and Computer Network Defense (CND),* CJCSI 6510.01D, June 15, 2004.

———, *Chairman of the Joint Chiefs of Staff Instruction: Joint Capabilities Integration and Development System,* CJCSI 3170.01E, May 11, 2005.

———, *Chairman of the Joint Chiefs of Staff Manual: Operation of the Joint Capabilities Integration and Development System,* CJCSM 3170.01B, May 11, 2005.

———, *Chairman of the Joint Chiefs of Staff Instruction: Rapid Validation and Resourcing of Joint Urgent Operational Needs (JUONs) in the Year of Execution,* CJCSI 3470.01, July 15, 2005.

———, *Chairman of the Joint Chiefs of Staff Instruction: Interoperability and Supportability of Information Technology and National Security Systems,* CJCSI 6212.01D, March 8, 2006, directive current as of March 14, 2007.

———, *Chairman of the Joint Chiefs of Staff Instruction: Joint Military Intelligence Requirements Certification,* CJCSI 3312.01A, February 23, 2007.

U.S. Joint Forces Command, *Joint Requirements Oversight Council Memorandum: Global Information Grid Capstone Requirements Document,* JROCM 134-01, August 30, 2001.

U.S. National Telecommunications and Information Administration, *Manual of Regulations and Procedures for Federal Radio Frequency Management,* Washington, D.C.: U.S. Department of Commerce and National Telecommunications and Information Administration, May 2003.

Bibliography

10 U.S. Code 2223, Information Technology: Additional Responsibilities of Chief Information Officers, October 1, 1998.

10 U.S. Code 2224, Defense Information Assurance Program, amended October 30, 2000.

ASD(NII)—*see* Office of the Assistant Secretary of Defense for Networks and Information Integration.

Assessment Panel of the Defense Acquisition Performance Assessment Project for the Deputy Secretary of Defense, *Defense Acquisition Performance Assessment: A Report by the Assessment Panel of the Defense Acquisition Performance Assessment Project for the Deputy Secretary of Defense*, Washington, D.C., 2006.

Bendel, Mike, *An Introduction to Department of Defense IA Certification and Accreditation Process (DIACAP)*, Washington, D.C.: Lunarline, March 1, 2006. As of June 21, 2007:
http://www.lunarline.com/docs/Lunarline_DIACAP_Process.pdf

Bowman, Tom, "Cost Climbs on Army's Contract with Boeing," *The Baltimore Sun*, April 30, 2005, p. A1.

Defense Information Systems Agency, Network Centric Operations and Warfare (NCOW)—Reference Model, July 2, 2003a.

———, "Global Information Grid (GIG) Architecture, Version 2.0," December 2003b.

Director, Washington Headquarters Service, U.S. Department of Defense, *Department of Defense Procedures for Management of Information Requirements*, DoD 8910.1-M, June 1998. As of June 21, 2007:
http://www.armyg1.army.mil/hr/weight/DoD%2089101-M%20Procedures%20for%20Mgmt%20of%20Info%20Reqmts.pdf

Director of Central Intelligence, *Director of Central Intelligence Directive: Security Policy for Sensitive Compartmented Information and Security Policy*, DCID 6/1, March 1, 1995, administratively updated November 4, 2003.

DITO—*see* U.S. Department of Defense Internet Protocol Version 6 Transition Office.

DoD—*see* U.S. Department of Defense.

DoD CIO—*see* U.S. Department of Defense Chief Information Officer.

DSB and OUSD(AT&L)—*see* U.S. Defense Science Board and U.S. Office of the Under Secretary of Defense for Acquisition, Technology, and Logistics.

Federal Information Security Management Act of 2002, 107th Congress, 2nd Session, House of Representatives bill 3844, March 5, 2002. As of June 21, 2007:
http://frwebgate.access.gpo.gov/cgi-bin/getdoc.cgi?dbname=107_cong_bills&docid=f:h3844ih.txt.pdf

Feickert, Andrew, *The Joint Tactical Radio System (JTRS) and the Army's Future Combat System (FCS): Issues for Congress*, Ft. Belvoir, Va.: Ft. Belvoir Defense Technical Information Center, 2005. As of July 31, 2007:
http://handle.dtic.mil/100.2/ADA443737

FISMA—*see* Public Law 107-347.

Hura, Myron, Gary McLeod, Lara Schmidt, Manuel Cohen, Mel Eisman, and Elliot Axelband, *Space Capabilities Document: Implications of Past and Current Efforts for Future Programs*, Santa Monica, Calif.: RAND Corporation, forthcoming. Not available to the general public.

IEEE Computer Society, *IEEE Standard Computer Dictionary: A Compilation of IEEE Standard Computer Glossaries*, New York: Institute of Electrical and Electronics Engineers, 1990.

JCS—*see* U.S. Joint Chiefs of Staff.

MCEB—*see* Military Communications-Electronics Board.

Military Communications-Electronics Board, *MCEB Organization, Mission and Functions Manual*, MCEB publication 1, March 1, 2002. As of June 21, 2007:
http://jitc.fhu.disa.mil/jitc_dri/pdfs/mceb_pub1.pdf

National Security Telecommunications and Information Systems Security Committee, *National Policy Governing the Acquisition of Information Assurance (IA) and IA-Enabled Information Technology (IT) Products*, NSTISSP 11, January 2000, revised June 2003.

Office of the Assistant Secretary of Defense for Networks and Information Integration, U.S. Department of Defense, "Temporary Suspension of the Joint Tactical Radio Systems (JTRS) Waive Process," May 23, 2005a.

———, "Information Support Plan (ISP) Acquisition Streamlining Pilot Program," memorandum for secretaries of the military departments, under secretaries of defense, assistant secretaries of defense, general counsel of the Department of Defense, inspector general of the Department of Defense, director of operational test and evaluation, assistants to the secretary of defense, director of administration and management, director of program analysis and evaluation, director of force transformation, directors of the defense agencies, director of the joint staff, and directors of the Department of Defense field activities, Washington, D.C., August 26, 2005b. As of June 21, 2007:
https://acc.dau.mil/GetAttachment.aspx?id=22221&pname=file&lang=en-US&aid=2140

Office of the Chief of Naval Operations, Department of the Navy, *Navy Information Assurance (IA) Program*, OPNAV instruction 5239.1B, November 9, 1999. As of August 21, 2007:
http://doni.daps.dla.mil/Directives/
05000%20General%20Management%20Security%20and%20Safety%20Services/
05-200%20Management%20Program%20and%20Techniques%20Services/5239.1B.pdf

Office of the Intelligence Community Chief Information Officer, "Top Secret/Sensitive Compartmented Information and Below Interoperability (TSABI) Policy," version 4.20, November 24, 2003.

Office of the Secretary, Department of the Navy, *Department of the Navy Information Assurance (IA) Policy*, SECNAV instruction 5239.3A, December 20, 2004. As of August 21, 2007:
http://doni.daps.dla.mil/Directives/
05000%20General%20Management%20Security%20and%20Safety%20Services/
05-200%20Management%20Program%20and%20Techniques%20Services/5239.3A.pdf

Office of the Under Secretary of Defense for Acquisition, Technology, and Logistics, *Department of Defense Manual: Defense Standardization Program (DSP) Policies and Procedures*, DoD 4120.24-M, March 2000. As of June 21, 2007:
http://www.dtic.mil/whs/directives/corres/pdf/412024m.pdf

———, *Operation of the Defense Acquisition System*, Fort Belvoir Defense Technical Information Center, DoDI 5000.2, 2003. As of June 21, 2007:
http://handle.dtic.mil/100.2/ADA434924

Office of the Under Secretary of Defense for Acquisition, Technology, and Logistics, and the Assistant Secretary of Defense for Command, Control, Communications, and Intelligence, "Clinger-Cohen Act Compliance Policy," memorandum for secretaries of the military departments, chair of the Joint Chiefs of Staff, under secretaries of defense, assistant secretaries of defense, general counsel of the Department of Defense, inspector general of the Department of Defense, and the directors of the defense agencies, March 8, 2002a. As of July 2, 2007:
http://www.acq.osd.mil/dpap/Docs/ar/Clinger-Cohen%20Acrobat%20Document.pdf

———, "Clinger-Cohen Act Compliance Policy for Major Automated Information Systems," memorandum for secretaries of the military departments, chair of the Joint Chiefs of Staff, under secretaries of defense, assistant secretaries of defense, general counsel of the Department of Defense, inspector general of the Department of Defense, and the directors of the defense agencies, June 19, 2002b. As of July 2, 2007:
http://acquisition.navy.mil/rda/content/download/873/3813/file/061902cca.pdf

OPNAV—*see* Office of the Chief of Naval Operations, Department of the Navy.

OUSD(AT&L)—*see* Office of the Under Secretary of Defense for Acquisition, Technology, and Logistics.

Public Law 104-106, National Defense Authorization Act for Fiscal Year 1996, January 3, 1996. As of June 21, 2007:
http://frwebgate.access.gpo.gov/cgi-bin/getdoc.cgi?dbname=104_cong_bills&docid=f:s1124enr.txt.pdf

Public Law 107-347, Federal Information Security Management Act of 2002, December 17, 2002.

Ross, Ron, Stu Katzke, Arnold Johnson, Marianne Swanson, Gary Stoneburner, George Rogers, and Annabelle Lee, *Recommended Security Controls for Federal Information Systems*, Gaithersburg, Md.: National Institute of Standards and Technology, NIST special publication 800-53, February 2005. As of June 21, 2007:
http://csrc.nist.gov/publications/nistpubs/800-53/SP800-53.pdf

SECNAV—*see* Office of the Secretary, Department of the Navy.

Staten, Roddy, policy analyst, Booz Allen Hamilton, "DoD Information Assurance Certification and Accreditation Process (DIACAP)/DIACAP Knowledge Service/Enterprise Mission Assurance Support Service (eMASS)," briefing, November 2005. As of June 21, 2007:
http://www.sdissa.org/downloads/Revised_DIACAP_KS_eMASS_Brief%20ISSA_10-28-05.ppt

U.S. Assistant Secretary of Defense, "Department of Defense (DoD) Public Key Infrastructure (PKI)," memorandum, May 21, 2002.

U.S. Assistant Secretary of Defense for Command, Control, Communications, and Intelligence, "Radio Acquisitions," memorandum, August 28, 1998.

———, *Department of Defense Directive: DoD Logistics Use of Electronic Data Interchange (EDI) Standards*, DoDD 8190.1, May 5, 2000. As of June 21, 2007:
http://www.dtic.mil/whs/directives/corres/pdf/819001p.pdf

———, "Approval of Commercial Off-the-Shelf Information Technology/National Security Systems Software Action Plan," memorandum, April 8, 2003.

U.S. Defense Science Board, and U.S. Office of the Under Secretary of Defense for Acquisition, Technology, and Logistics, *Defense Science Board Summer Study on Transformation: A Progress Assessment*, Vol. 1, Washington, D.C.: Office of the Under Secretary of Defense for Acquisition, Technology, and Logistics, 2006.

U.S. Department of Defense, *Department of Defense Directive: Management and Use of the Radio Frequency Spectrum*, DoDD 4650.1, June 24, 1987.

———, *Department of Defense Instruction: DoD Information Technology Security Certification and Accreditation Process (DITSCAP)*, DoDI 5200.40, December 30, 1997. As of June 21, 2007:
http://www.dtic.mil/whs/directives/corres/pdf/520040p.pdf

———, *Department of Defense Directive: Military Communications-Electronics Board (MCEB)*, DoDD 5100.35, March 10, 1998a. As of June 21, 2007:
http://www.dtic.mil/whs/directives/corres/pdf/510035p.pdf

———, *Department of Defense Instruction: Defense Standardization Program (DSP)*, DoDI 4120.24, June 18, 1998b, administrative reissuance incorporating change 1, March 9, 2000. As of June 21, 2007:
http://www.dtic.mil/whs/directives/corres/pdf/412024p.pdf

———, *Department of Defense Directive: DoD Logistics Use of Electronic Data Interchange (EDI) Standards*, DoDD 8190.1, May 5, 2000. As of June 21, 2007:
http://www.dtic.mil/whs/directives/corres/pdf/819001p.pdf

———, *Global Information Grid Capstone Requirements Document*, JROCM 134-01, August 30, 2001.

———, *Department of Defense Directive: The Department of Defense (DoD) Electronic Business/Electronic Commerce (EB/EC) Program*, DoDD 8190.2, June 23, 2002a. As of June 21, 2007:
http://www.nsa.gov/business/busin00007.pdf

———, *Department of Defense Directive: Smart Card Technology*, DoDD 8190.3, August 31, 2002b. As of June 21, 2007:
https://www.cac.mil/assets/pdfs/DoDD_81903.pdf

———, *Department of Defense Directive: Global Information Grid (GIG) Overarching Policy*, DoDD 8100.1, September 19, 2002c, certified current through November 21, 2003. As of June 21, 2007:
http://www.dtic.mil/whs/directives/corres/pdf/810001p.pdf

———, *Department of Defense Directive: Information Assurance (IA)*, DoDD 8500.1, October 24, 2002d. As of June 21, 2007:
https://www.cac.mil/assets/pdfs/DoDD_8500.1.pdf

———, *Joint Battle Management Command and Control*, MID 912, January 7, 2003a.

———, *Department of Defense Instruction: Information Assurance (IA) Implementation*, DoDI 8500.2, February 6, 2003b. As of June 21, 2007:
https://www.cac.mil/assets/pdfs/DoDD_8500.2.pdf

———, *Department of Defense Net-Centric Data Strategy*, Washington, D.C., May 9, 2003c. As of June 21, 2007:
http://www.defenselink.mil/cio-nii/docs/Net-Centric-Data-Strategy-2003-05-092.pdf

———, *Department of Defense Instruction: Operation of the Defense Acquisition System*, DoDI 5000.2, May 12, 2003c. As of June 21, 2007:
http://www.acq.osd.mil/dpap/Docs/new/5000.2%2005-12-06.pdf

———, *Department of Defense Architecture Framework*, version 1.0, August 30, 2003d.

———, *National Security Space Acquisition Policy: Guidance for DoD Space System Acquisition Process*, NSSAP 03-01, October 6, 2003e.

———, *Defense Acquisition Guidebook*, Washington, D.C.: U.S. Department of Defense, 2004a. As of June 21, 2007:
http://purl.access.gpo.gov/GPO/LPS55065

———, *Department of Defense Instruction: Department of Defense (DOD) Voice Networks*, DoDI 8100.3, January 16, 2004b. As of June 21, 2007:
http://jitc.fhu.disa.mil/jitc_dri/pdfs/di81003p.pdf

———, *Department of Defense Instruction: Multinational Information Sharing Networks Implementation*, DoDI 8110.1, February 6, 2004c. As of June 21, 2007:
http://www.dtic.mil/whs/directives/corres/pdf/811001p.pdf

———, *Department of Defense Directive: Use of Commercial Wireless Devices, Services, and Technologies in the Department of Defense (DoD) Global Information Grid (GIG)*, DoDD 8100.2, April 14, 2004d. As of June 21, 2007:
https://acc.dau.mil/GetAttachment.aspx?id=18141&pname=file&aid=639

———, *Department of Defense Directive: Interoperability and Supportability of Information Technology (IT) and National Security Systems (NSS)*, DoDD 4630.5, May 5, 2004e.

———, *Department of Defense Directive: DoD Executive Agent for Information Technology Standards*, DoDD 5101.7, May 21, 2004f, certified current as of November 3, 2006.

———, *Department of Defense Instruction: Procedures for Interoperability and Supportability of Information Technology (IT) and National Security Systems (NSS)*, DoDI 4630.8, June 30, 2004g. As of June 21, 2007:
http://www.dtic.mil/whs/directives/corres/pdf/463008p.pdf

———, "Net-Centric IA Strategy," June 30, 2004h.

———, *Department of Defense Instruction: Information Assurance (IA) in the Defense Acquisition System*, DoDI 8580.1, July 9, 2004i. As of June 21, 2007:
http://www.dtic.mil/whs/directives/corres/pdf/858001p.pdf

———, *Department of Defense Instruction: Ports, Protocols, and Services Management (PPSM)*, DoDI 8551.1, August 13, 2004j. As of June 21, 2007:
http://www.dtic.mil/whs/directives/corres/pdf/855101p.pdf

———, *Department of Defense Directive: DoD Electromagnetic Environmental Effects (E3) Program*, DoDD 3222.3, September 8, 2004k. As of June 21, 2007:
http://www.dtic.mil/whs/directives/corres/pdf/322203p.pdf

———, *Department of Defense Directive: Data Sharing in a Net-Centric Department of Defense*, DoDD 8320.02, December 2, 2004l, certified current as of April 23, 2007. As of June 21, 2007:
http://www.dtic.mil/whs/directives/corres/pdf/832002p.pdf

———, *Department of Defense Directive: Information Assurance (IA) Policy for Space Systems Used by the Department of Defense*, DoDD 8581.1E, June 21, 2005a. As of June 21, 2007:
http://www.dtic.mil/whs/directives/corres/pdf/858101p.pdf

———, *Department of Defense Directive: Defense Critical Infrastructure Program (DCIP)*, DoDD 3020.40, August 19, 2005b. As of June 21, 2007:
http://www.dtic.mil/whs/directives/corres/pdf/302040p.pdf

———, *Department of Defense Directive: Information Technology Portfolio Management*, DoDD 8115.01, October 10, 2005c. As of June 21, 2007:
http://www.dtic.mil/whs/directives/corres/pdf/811501p.pdf

———, *Department of Defense Instruction: Department of Defense Information Assurance Certification and Accreditation Process (DIACAP)*, DoDI 8510.bb, July 2006a.

———, *Defense Acquisition Guidebook*, Washington, D.C.: U.S. Department of Defense, July 24, 2006b. As of July 2, 2007:
http://purl.access.gpo.gov/GPO/LPS55065

———, "End-to-End IA Component of the GIG Integrated Architecture," October 26, 2006c.

U.S. Department of Defense Chief Information Officer, "Department of Defense Global Information Grid Information Assurance," guidance and policy memorandum 6-8510, June 2000a.

———, "GIG Networks," guidance and policy memorandum 4-8460, August 24, 2000b.

———, "Global Information Grid (GIG) Computing," guidance and policy memorandum 11-8450, April 6, 2001.

———, "DoD Net-Centric Data Strategy," memorandum for secretaries of the military departments, chair of the Joint Chiefs of Staff, under secretaries of defense, director of defense research and evaluation, assistant secretaries of defense, general counsel of the U.S. Department of Defense, inspector general of the U.S. Department of Defense, director of operational test and evaluation, assistants to the secretary of defense, director of administration and management, director of force transformation, director of net assessment, directors of the defense agencies, and directors of U.S. Department of Defense field activities, May 9, 2003. As of June 21, 2007:
http://www.defenselink.mil/cio-nii/docs/Net-Centric-Data-Strategy-2003-05-092.pdf

———, "Interim Department of Defense (DoD) Information Assurance (IA) Certification and Accreditation (C&A) Process Guidance," memorandum, July 6, 2007.

U.S. Department of Defense Deputy Chief Information Officer, "Department of Defense Information Technology (IT) Registry Interim Guidance," memorandum, March 17, 2003.

U.S. Department of Defense Information Technology Standards Registry (DISR) baseline release.

U.S. Department of Defense Internet Protocol Version 6 Transition Office, "DoD CIO Memo, IPv6 Interim Transition Guidance," September 29, 2003.

U.S. Deputy Secretary of Defense, "DoD Chief Information Officer (CIO) Guidance and Policy Memorandum No. 8-8001—March 31, 2000—Global Information Grid," memorandum for secretaries of the military departments; chair of the Joint Chiefs of Staff; under secretaries of defense; director of defense research and engineering; assistant secretaries of defense; general counsel of the Department of Defense; inspector general of the Department of Defense; director of operational test and evaluation; commanders of the Combatant Command; assistants to the secretary of defense; director of administration and management; directors of the defense agencies; director of the National Reconnaissance Office; directors of Department of Defense field activities; chief information officers of the military departments; director of the joint staff for command, control, communication, and computer systems; chief information officers of the defense agencies;

director of the intelligence community management staff; and the intelligence community chief information officer, March 31, 2000.

U.S. Joint Chiefs of Staff, *Department of Defense Dictionary of Military and Associated Terms*, Washington, D.C.: Joint Chiefs of Staff, March 23, 1994, as amended April 6, 1999.

————, *Chairman of the Joint Chiefs of Staff Instruction: Theater Joint Tactical Networks Configuration Control Board Charter*, CJCSI 5122.01B, August 23, 2001.

————, *Chairman of the Joint Chiefs of Staff Instruction: NAVSTAR Global Positioning System Selective Availability Anti-Spoofing Module Requirements*, CJCSI 6140.01A, March 31, 2004a.

————, *Chairman of the Joint Chiefs of Staff Instruction: Information Assurance (IA) and Computer Network Defense (CND)*, CJCSI 6510.01D, June 15, 2004b.

————, *Chairman of the Joint Chiefs of Staff Instruction: Joint Capabilities Integration and Development System*, CJCSI 3170.01E, May 11, 2005a.

————, *Chairman of the Joint Chiefs of Staff Manual: Operation of the Joint Capabilities Integration and Development System*, CJCSM 3170.01B, May 11, 2005b.

————, *Chairman of the Joint Chiefs of Staff Instruction: Rapid Validation and Resourcing of Joint Urgent Operational Needs (JUONs) in the Year of Execution*, CJCSI 3470.01, July 15, 2005c.

————, *Chairman of the Joint Chiefs of Staff Instruction: Interoperability and Supportability of Information Technology and National Security Systems*, CJCSI 6212.01D, March 8, 2006, directive current as of March 14, 2007. As of June 21, 2007:
http://www.dtic.mil/cjcs_directives/cdata/unlimit/6212_01.pdf

————, *Chairman of the Joint Chiefs of Staff Instruction: Joint Military Intelligence Requirements Certification*, CJCSI 3312.01A, February 23, 2007. As of June 21, 2007:
http://www.dtic.mil/cjcs_directives/cdata/unlimit/3312_01.pdf

U.S. Joint Forces Command, *Joint Requirements Oversight Council Memorandum: Global Information Grid Capstone Requirements Document*, JROCM 134-01, August 30, 2001.

U.S. National Telecommunications and Information Administration, *Manual of Regulations and Procedures for Federal Radio Frequency Management*, Washington, D.C.: U.S. Department of Commerce and National Telecommunications and Information Administration, May 2003. As of June 21, 2007:
http://purl.access.gpo.gov/GPO/LPS47198

Wierum, Jenifer M., *Defense Information Assurance Certification and Accreditation Process (DIACAP) and the Global Information Grid (GIG) Information Assurance (IA) Architecture*, McLean, Va.: CygnaCom Solutions, March 2005. As of June 21, 2007:
http://www.afei.org/documents/DIACAPandtheGIGCCRTS_371.pdf